Cuban Anarchism
The History of a Movement

by
Frank Fernández

Translated by
Charles Bufe

See Sharp Press ◆ Tucson, Arizona ◆ 2001

Copyright © 2001 by Frank Fernández.
Translation copyright © 2001 by Charles Bufe.
All rights reserved.
For information contact See Sharp Press,
P.O. Box 1731, Tucson, AZ 85702-1731.
Web site: www.seesharppress.com
Free catalog upon request.

Fernández, Frank.
    Cuban anarchism : the history of a movement / Frank Fernández ;
introduction by Chaz Bufe. – Tucson, Ariz. : See Sharp Press, 2001.
        154 p. : ill. ; 23 cm.
        Includes bibliographical references and index.
        ISBN 1-884365-19-1
        1. Cuba - Politics and government. 2. Anarchism - Cuba - History.
3. Anarchists - Cuba - History 4. Syndicalism - Cuba - History.
5. Labor movement - Cuba - History. 6. Trade-unions - Cuba - History.
7. Trade-unions and communism - Cuba - History. I. Title.
                335.83097291

First Edition

Cover design by Clifford Harper. Interior design by Chaz Bufe. Printed in USA by
Thomson-Shore, Inc. on acid-free paper with soy-based ink .

Dedicated to the memory of Maria Teresa

Dearly beloved and sorely missed

Your patience and love will

Live in our hearts

Contents

Introduction

This is not a conventional history. Rather, it's a tribute, an homage to the thousands of Cuban anarchists who worked over the course of more than a century to build a freer, juster world, and who, but for this book, would remain almost entirely forgotten. That would be a tragedy, as virtually all of them were idealistic, admirable human beings, and many were truly heroic. All are more deserving of historical remembrance than such power-hungry dictators as Gerardo Machado, Fulgencio Batista, and Fidel Castro.

The author of this work, Frank Fernández, has been a member of the Movimiento Libertario Cubano en el Exilio (MLCE) for decades, and was the editor of its long-running periodical, *Guángara Libertaria*,[1] for which he wrote easily half a million, and perhaps a million, words on Cuban history and politics. He is also the author of the book, *La sangre de Santa Águeda,* which deals with a pivotal event in Spanish and Cuban history, the assassination of the Spanish premier Cánovas del Castillo in 1897.

Like the other members of the MLCE and their predecessors in Cuba, Frank has done his political work in his "spare" time—after his day job as a mechanical engineer—and has never received a dime for his countless hours of work on behalf of Cuban freedom. He writes here from deep conviction and also from a deep knowledge of the history of Cuba and its anarchist movement. That knowledge includes personal acquaintance with most of the Cuban anarchists mentioned in chapters 4 and 5, whose testimony and remembrances form the backbone of those chapters.

In reading this history of Cuban anarchism, one is struck both by the immense courage and dedication of the Cuban anarchists, and by the lessons to be learned from their struggles. A particularly poignant lesson is that concerning so-called wars of national liberation. In the 1890s, Cuba's large and powerful anarchist movement split over the question of whether or not to participate in the national independence struggle. A great many anarchists defected to the independence movement, but that movement proved to be a disaster both for the anarchists, who were seriously weakened, and for Cuba's people

---

1. "Guángara" is a Cubanism meaning a sharp jest or jape.

as a whole, hundreds of thousands of whom died in the conflict. In the end, nothing worthwhile was achieved—Spanish colonialism was replaced, but by a republic in the hands of the sugar barons and beholden to foreign financial interests. At least some Cuban anarchists evidently learned from this fiasco—that it's always a mistake for anarchists to put aside their principles and support would-be governors, no matter how "nationalist" or "progressive"—but a great many other anarchists evidently didn't.

Twenty years after this Cuban disaster, large numbers of the world's anarchists (including many Cubans) threw their support to the Bolshevik government after the 1917 Russian revolution. Despite growing evidence of the brutal, totalitarian nature of the Communist regime, many anarchists continued to support it until well into the 1920s, when two well known and respected anarchists, Alexander Berkman (in *The Russian Tragedy* and *The Bolshevik Myth*) and Emma Goldman (in *My Disillusionment in Russia* and *My Further Disillusionment in Russia*) revealed the truth. Even then, some anarchists refused to surrender their illusions about the nature of the "workers' state."

This situation repeated itself with Castro's rise to power in 1959. A great many anarchists, especially in Europe, were so desperate to see positive social change that they saw it where there was none—in Cuba, thanks in part to a skilled disinformation campaign by Castro's propaganda apparatus. Despite suppression of civil liberties, the prohibition of independent political activity, the government takeover of the unions, the militarization of the economy, the gradual impoverishment of the country (despite massive Soviet economic aid), the reemergence of a class system, the institution of a network of political spies in every neighborhood (the so-called Committees for the Defense of the Revolution), and the government-fostered personality cults which grew up around Fidel Castro and Ernesto ("Che") Guevara, large and important sections of the world's anarchist movement supported Castro until well into the 1970s.

That situation began to change in 1976 with publication of the respected American anarchist Sam Dolgoff's *The Cuban Revolution: A Critical Perspective.* But even today some anarchists continue to be hoodwinked by the Castro regime's "revolutionary" rhetoric and the veneer of social welfare measures with which it covers its ruthless determination to cling to power at any price.

The Cuban experience provides us with valuable lessons. Two of the most important are that anarchists should *never* support marxist regimes, and that they should be extremely wary about supporting, let alone participating in, so-called wars of national liberation. These are the negative lessons to be learned from the history of Cuba's anarchists. The positive lesson is that it is possible to build a large, powerful revolutionary movement, despite lack of physical resources, through dedication and hard work.

Before going on to the body of this book, it's necessary to consider the ideology of Cuba's anarchists. Because there are so many popular misconceptions about anarchism, it's imperative to clarify what anarchism is and what it isn't. First, what it isn't:

Anarchism is not terrorism. An overwhelming majority of anarchists have always rejected terrorism, because they've been intelligent enough to realize that means determine ends, that terrorism is inherently vanguardist, and that even when "successful" it almost always leads to bad results. The anonymous authors of *You Can't Blow Up a Social Relationship: The Anarchist Case Against Terrorism* put it like this:

> The total collapse of this society would provide no guarantee about what replaced it. Unless a majority of people had the ideas and organization sufficient for the creation of an alternative society, we would see the old world reassert itself because it is what people would be used to, what they believed in, what existed unchallenged in their own personalities.
>
> Proponents of terrorism and guerrillaism are to be opposed because their actions are vanguardist and authoritarian, because their ideas, to the extent that they are substantial, are wrong or unrelated to the results of their actions (especially when they call themselves libertarians or anarchists), because their killing cannot be justified, and finally because their actions produce either repression with nothing in return, or an authoritarian regime.

Decades of government and corporate slander cannot alter this reality: the overwhelming majority of anarchists reject terrorism for both practical and ethical reasons. *Time* magazine recently called Ted Kaczynski "the king of the anarchists," but that doesn't make it so; *Time*'s words are just another typical, perhaps deliberately dishonest, attempt to tar all anarchists with the terrorist brush.

This is not to say that armed resistance is never appropriate. Clearly there are situations in which one has little choice, as when facing a dictatorship that suppresses civil liberties and prevents one from acting openly—which has happened repeatedly in Cuba. Even then, armed resistance should be undertaken reluctantly and as a last resort, because violence is inherently undesirable due to the suffering it causes; because it provides repressive regimes excuses for further repression; because it provides them with the opportunity to commit atrocities against civilians and to blame those atrocities on their "terrorist" opponents (as has happened recently in Algeria); and because, as history has shown, the chances of even limited success are quite low.

Even though armed resistance may sometimes be called for in repressive situations, it's a far different matter to succumb to the romance of the gun and to engage in urban guerrilla warfare in relatively open societies in which civil liberties are largely intact and in which one does not have mass popular support at the start of one's violent campaign. Violence in such situations does little but drive the public into the "protective" arms of the government; it narrows political dialogue (tending to polarize the populace into pro- and anti-guerrilla factions); it turn politics into a spectator sport for the vast majority of people;[2] it provides the government with a handy excuse to suppress civil liberties; and it induces the onset of repressive regimes, "better" able to handle the "terrorist" problem than their more tolerant predecessors. It's also worth mentioning that the chances of success of such violent, vanguardist campaigns are microscopic. They are simply arrogant, ill-thought-out roads to disaster.[3]

Anarchism is not primitivism. In recent decades, groups of quasi-religious mystics have begun equating the primitivism they advocate (rejection of "technology," whatever that might mean) with anarchism.[4] In reality, the two have nothing to do with each other, as we'll see when we consider what anarchism actually is—a set of philosophical/ethical precepts and organizational principles designed to maximize human freedom.

For now, suffice it to say that the elimination of technology advocated by primitivist groups would inevitably entail the deaths of literally billions of human beings in a world utterly dependent upon interlocking technologies for everything from food production and delivery to communications to medical treatment. This fervently desired outcome, the elimination of technology, could only occur

---

2. It may be that now due to apathy, but in violent/repressive situations other options are cut off for almost everyone not directly involved in armed resistance.

3. For further discussion of this matter, see *You Can't Blow Up a Social Relationship: The Anarchist Case Against Terrorism*, available from See Sharp Press (the publisher of this book). See also *Bourgeois Influences on Anarchism*, by Luigi Fabbri, now published by Left Bank Distribution.

4. Ted Kaczynski is in some ways quite typical of this breed of romantic. He differs from most of them in that he acted on his beliefs (albeit in a cowardly, violent manner) and in that he actually lived a relatively primitive existence in the backwoods of Montana—unlike most of his co-religionists, who live comfortably in urban areas and employ the technology they profess to loathe.

through means which are the absolute antithesis of anarchism: the use of coercion and violence on a mass scale.[5]

Anarchism is not chaos; Anarchism is not rejection of organization. This is another popular misconception, repeated *ad nauseam* by the media and by anarchism's political foes, especially marxists (who sometimes know better). Even a brief look at the works of anarchism's leading theoreticians and writers confirms that this belief is in error. Over and over in the writings of Proudhon, Bakunin, Kropotkin, Rocker, Ward, Bookchin, et al., one finds not a rejection of organization, but rather a preoccupation with how society should be organized in accord with the anarchist principles of individual freedom and social justice. For a century and a half now, anarchists have been arguing that coercive, hierarchical organization (as embodied in government) is *not* equivalent to organization *per se* (which they regard as necessary), and that coercive organization should be replaced by decentralized, nonhierarchical organization based on voluntary cooperation and mutual aid. This is hardly a rejection of organization.

Anarchism is not amoral egotism. As does any avant garde social movement, anarchism attracts more than its share of flakes, parasites, and sociopaths, persons simply looking for a glamorous label to cover their often-pathological selfishness, their disregard for the rights and dignity of others, and their pathetic desire to be the center of attention. These individuals tend to give anarchism a bad name, because even though they have very little in common with actual anarchists—that is, persons concerned with ethical behavior, social justice, and the rights of both themselves *and others*—they're often quite exhibitionistic, and their disreputable actions sometimes come into the public eye. To make matters worse, these exhibitionists sometimes publish their self-glorifying views and deliberately misidentify those views as "anarchist." To cite an example, the publisher of a pretentiously (sub)titled American "anarchist" journal recently published a book by a fellow egotist consisting largely of *ad hominem* attacks on actual anarchists—knowing full well that the "anarchist" author of the book was a notorious police narcotics informant. Such individuals may (mis)use the label, but they're anarchists only in the sense that the now-defunct German Democratic Republic (East Germany) was democratic and a republic.

This is what anarchism isn't. This is what it is:

In its narrowest sense, anarchism is simply the rejection of the state, the rejection of coercive government. Under this extremely

5. For further discussion of this topic, see the "Primitive Thought" appendix to *Listen Anarchist!*, available from See Sharp Press.

narrow definition, even such apparent absurdities as "anarcho-capitalism" and religious anarchism are possible.[6]

But most anarchists use the term "anarchism" in a much broader sense, defining it as the rejection of coercion and domination in all forms. So, most anarchists reject not only coercive government, but also religion and capitalism, which they see as other forms of the twin evils, domination and coercion. They reject religion because they see it as the ultimate form of domination, in which a supposedly all-powerful god hands down "thou shalts" and "thou shalt nots" to its "flock." They likewise reject capitalism because it's designed to produce rich and poor, because it inevitably produces a system of domination in which some give orders and others have little choice but to take them. For similar reasons, on a personal level almost all anarchists reject sexism, racism, and homophobia—all of which produce artificial inequality, and thus domination.

To put this another way, anarchists believe in freedom in both its negative and positive senses. In this country, freedom is routinely presented only in its negative sense, that of being free *from* restraint. Hence most people equate freedom only with such things as freedom of speech, freedom of association, and freedom of (or from) religion. But there's also a positive aspect of freedom, an aspect which anarchists almost alone insist on.

That positive aspect is what Emma Goldman called the freedom *to*. And that freedom, the freedom of action, the freedom to enjoy or use, is highly dependent upon access to the world's resources. Because of this the rich are, in a very real sense, free to a much greater degree than the rest of us. To cite an example in the area of free speech, Donald Trump could easily buy dozens of daily news-papers or television stations to propagate his views and influence public opinion. How many working people could do the same? How many working people could afford to buy a single daily newspaper or a single television station? The answer is obvious. Working people cannot do such things; instead, they're reduced to producing 'zines with a readership of a few hundred persons or putting up pages on the Internet in their relatively few hours of free time.

---

6. Indeed, there have been a fairly large number of admirable religious anarchists, individuals such as Leo Tolstoy and Dorothy Day (and the members of her Catholic Worker groups, such as Ammon Hennacy), though to most anarchists advocating freedom on Earth while bowing to a heavenly tyrant (no matter how imaginary) seems an insupportable contradiction.

To the best of my knowledge, there have been no such shining examples of anarcho-capitalists.

Examples of the greater freedom of the rich abound in daily life. To put this in general terms, because they do not have to work, the rich not only have far more money (that is, more access to resources) but also far more time to pursue their interests, pleasures, and desires than do the rest of us. To cite a concrete example, the rich are free to send their children to the best colleges employing the best instructors, while the rest of us, if we can afford college at all, make do with community and state colleges employing slave-labor "adjunct faculty" and overworked, underpaid graduate-student teaching assistants. Once in college, the children of the rich are entirely free to pursue their studies, while most other students must work at least part time to support themselves, which deprives them of many hours which could be devoted to study. If you think about it, you can easily find additional examples of the greater freedom of the rich in the areas of medical care, housing, nutrition, travel, etc., etc.—in fact, in virtually every area of life.

This greater freedom of action of the rich comes at the expense of everyone else, through the diminishment of everyone else's freedom of action. There is no way around this, given that freedom of action is to a great extent determined by access to finite resources. Anatole France well illustrated the differences between the restrictions placed upon the rich and the poor when he wrote, "The law, in its majestic equality, forbids the rich as well as the poor to sleep under bridges, to beg in the streets, and to steal bread."

Because the primary goal of anarchism is the greatest possible amount of freedom for all, anarchists insist on equal freedom in both its negative and positive senses—that, in the negative sense, individuals be free to do whatever they wish as long as they do not harm or directly intrude on others; and, in the positive sense, that all individuals have equal freedom to act, that they have equal access to the world's resources.

Anarchists recognize that absolute freedom is an impossibility. What they argue for is that everyone have equal freedom from restraint (limited only by respect for the rights of others) and that everyone have as nearly as possible equal access to resources, thus ensuring equal (or near-equal) freedom to act.

This is anarchism in its theoretical sense.[7]

---

7. Of course, this discussion of anarchism is necessarily schematic, given that it's but a portion of the introduction to a short book. For elaboration, see many of the works listed in the bibliography, especially *Anarchism and Anarcho-syndicalism*, by Rudolf Rocker; *ABC of Anarchism*, by Alexander Berkman; *Fields, Factories and Workshops Tomorrow*, by Peter Kropotkin; and *Anarchy in Action*, by Colin Ward.

In Cuba, as in Spain and a few other countries, there have been serious attempts to make this theory reality through the movement known as anarcho-syndicalism. The primary purpose of anarcho-syndicalism is the replacement of coercive government by voluntary cooperation in the form of worker-controlled unions coordinating the entire economy. This would not only eliminate the main restraint on the negative freedoms (government), but would also be a huge step toward achieving positive freedom (the freedom *to*). The nearest this vision has ever come to fruition was in the Spanish Revolution, 1936–1939, when large areas of Spain, including its most heavily industrialized region, Catalonia, came under the control of the anarcho-syndicalist Confederación Nacional del Trabajo. George Orwell describes this achievement in *Homage to Catalonia*:

> The Anarchists were still in virtual control of Catalonia and the revolution was in full swing. . . . the aspect of Barcelona was something startling and overwhelming. It was the first time that I had ever been in a town where the working class was in the saddle. Practically every building of any size had been seized by the workers and was draped with red flags or with the red and black flag of the anarchists; . . . Every shop and café had an inscription saying it had been collectivized; even the bootblacks had been collectivized and their boxes painted red and black. Waiters and shop-workers looked you in the face and treated you as an equal. Servile and even ceremonial forms of speech had temporarily disappeared. . . . The revolutionary posters were everywhere, flaming from the walls in clean reds and blues that made the few remaining advertisements look like daubs of mud. . . . All this was queer and moving. There was much in it that I did not understand, in some ways I did not even like it, but I recognized it immediately as a state of affairs worth fighting for.

This is what the Cuban anarchists were fighting for. While they did not achieve what their Spanish comrades did, they built one of the largest anarcho-syndicalist movements the world has ever seen, which at its height in the 1920s included 80,000 to 100,000 workers in unions operated on anarchist principles.

This achievement did not come without cost: countless Cuban anarchists paid for it with their lives, imprisonment, or exile.

This is their story.

—Chaz Bufe, Tucson, Arizona

A Note on Terminology

Throughout the text the author uses the term "libertarian" in its original sense: as a synonym for "anarchist." Indeed, it was used almost exclusively in this sense until the 1970s when, in the United States, it was appropriated by the grossly misnamed Libertarian Party. This party has almost nothing to do with anarchist concepts of liberty, especially the concepts of equal freedom and positive freedom—the access to resources necessary to the freedom to act. Instead, this "Libertarian" party concerns itself exclusively with the negative freedoms, pretending that liberty exists only in the negative sense, while it simultaneously revels in the denial of equal positive freedom to the vast majority of the world's people. These "Libertarians" not only glorify capitalism, the mechanism that denies both equal freedom and positive freedom to the vast majority, but they also wish to retain the coercive apparatus of the state while eliminating its social welfare functions—hence widening the rift between rich and poor, and increasing the freedom of the rich by diminishing that of the poor (while keeping the boot of the state on their necks).

Thus, in the United States, the once exceedingly useful term "libertarian" has been hijacked by egotists who are in fact enemies of liberty in the full sense of the word. Fortunately, in the rest of the world, especially in the Spanish-speaking countries, "libertarian" ("libertario") remains a synonym for "anarchist." It is used in that sense in this book.

A Note on the Translation

There are major discrepancies between this English translation and the Spanish-language version of this book, *El anarquismo en Cuba,* published by Fundación de Estudios Libertarios Anselmo Lorenzo (more familiarly, Fundación Anselmo Lorenzo—FAL) in Madrid. There are four reasons for this: 1) I worked from the manuscript rather than from the published book; 2) I edited while I translated, and my editing changes were almost certainly quite different from those of the FAL editor(s); 3) I always attempted to preserve the meaning of the text, but often strayed from a literal translation; and 4) I asked the author to expand the text considerably, and he did so; he added several thousand words beyond what appears in *El anarquismo en Cuba.*

—CB

Preface

"This work is a brief overview of the influence that libertarian ideas have had upon the Cuban people. We believe that we have the duty to faithfully report the annals of the Cuban anarchists, who for more than a century have struggled and sacrificed in defense of liberty and for the interests of the most downtrodden classes in our society. We will briefly review the actions of a group of men and women who, totally without resources, without aid or protection, and who were forgotten and persecuted, not only influenced the history of the working class and campesinos, but also the history of the entire Cuban people."

These are the opening words in my pamphlet, *Cuba, The Anarchists & Liberty*, which was first published in English in 1987 by Monty Miller Press, and which has been reprinted since then by various groups, most recently appearing in electronic form on the Internet. It provides the basis of this small book. The emphasis in the present work lies in the final chapters, in which I deal with the last years of organized anarchism in Cuba, covering a series of incidents and events which were not included in the pamphlet.

As was to be expected, given its wide distribution, marxist and pro-Castro critics attempted to discredit my pamphlet. The least cynical accused me of producing an apologetic "panegyric" whose purpose was propagandistic. This is untrue. While I am an anarchist and the pamphlet certainly was pro-anarchist, it's right and proper that every social group promulgate its own "historical truth," as long as that interpretation is based in verifiable facts. That was my purpose and method in *Cuba, the Anarchists & Liberty*, and it continues to be so in the present work.

I would like to thank the last survivors of the Cuban anarchist movement—now spread across the diaspora—who have helped to make this project possible. Suria Liunsaín, Claudio Martínez, León G. Montelongo, and Helio Nardo collaborated on the final chapters. I also received assistance from several persons no longer on the scene: Marcelo Salinas, Casto Moscú, Manuel Ferro, Manuel González, Agustín Castro, Abelardo Iglesias, and Santiago Cobo. All of them contributed their memories to this work.

Finally, this book is dedicated in its entirety to all those anonymous militants whose names do not appear here, but whose selfless example made an ineradicable impression on our national destiny. Without them this history could never have been written.

—Frank Fernández, Miami, Florida

Organizations & Acronyms

AIT	Asociación Internacional de los Trabajadores
ALC	Asociación Libertaria de Cuba
ARS	Alianza Revolucionaria Socialista
BIL	Boletín de Información Libertaria
CDR	Comités en Defensa de la Revolución
CGT	Confederación General de Trabajadores
CNOC	Confederación Nacional Obrera de Cuba
CNT	Confederación Nacional del Trabajo
CO	Comisiones Obreras
CONI	Comité Obrero Nacional Independiente
CTC	Confederación de Trabajadores de Cuba
CTCR	Confederación de Trabajadores de Cuba Revolucionaria
DDG	Documento de Gaona
FAI	Federación Anarquista Ibérica
FAIT	Federazione Anarchica Italiana
FAL	Fundación Anselmo Lorenzo
FGAC	Federación de Grupos Anarquistas de Cuba
FJLC	Federación de Juventudes Libertarias de Cuba
FOH	Federación Obrera de La Habana
FRE	Federación Regional Española
FTC	Federación de Trabajadores de Cuba
ISHSS	International Society for Historical and Social Studies
IWA	International Workingmen's Association
IWW	Industrial Workers of the World
MAS	Movimiento de Acción Sindical
MLCE	Movimiento Libertario Cubano en el Exilio
M26J	Movimiento 26 de Julio
PCC	Partido Comunista Cubano
PLA	Partido Liberal Autonomista
PRC	Partido Revolucionario Cubano
PRCA	Partido Revolucionario Cubano Auténtico
PSP	Partido Socialista Popular
SAC	Sveriges Arbetares Centralorganisation
SGT	Sociedad General de Trabajadores
SIA	Solidaridad Internacional Antifascista

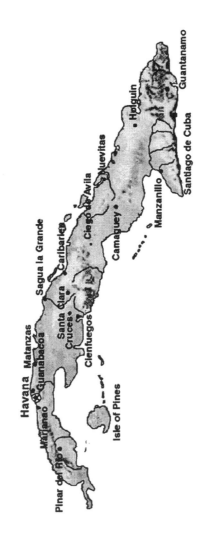

1

Colonialism & Separatism

(1865–1898)

Nineteenth-century Cuban society possessed a set of characteristics unique in the western hemisphere. From the beginning of the century, exploitation of Cuba's economic wealth had been the work of the white ruling class, who bore titles of Spanish nobility. This creole[1] aristocracy had enough power and resources to influence Spanish policy during the colonial epoch. While the rest of Latin America was violently freeing itself of Spanish colonialism, Cuba's creole plutocracy considered itself more Spanish than Fernando VII, the king of Spain, and very deliberately opposed any type of reformism, no matter how modest.

The cultivation of sugar cane, tobacco, and coffee was the basis of Cuba's agricultural abundance, and in order to compete in international markets Cuba's elite needed cheap labor. So, in open collusion with the Spanish crown and the colonial authorities, Cuba's plutocrats engaged in the massive importation of African slaves, in the process establishing an abusive, slavery-based society. By the middle of the 19th century, Cuba's aristocracy had become powerful sugar barons and Cuba's economy was abnormally dependent—by Latin American standards—on the slave trade and the institution of slavery.

The class structure of Cuban society was pyramidal in these years: on the top, the sugar barons and the Spanish colonial officials; in the middle, artisans, industrial, sugar and tobacco workers, including free blacks and campesinos; and on the bottom, black slaves. The division between the bottom two classes was not always clear cut despite the many racial and social divisions in Cuban society: campesinos and poor Spanish immigrants could suffer almost the same discrimination and exploitation as black slaves. It is well to keep in mind that these divisions in Cuban society were imposed by the dominant class and not by the people at the base of the social pyramid.

---

1. Cuban-born whites of Spanish ancestry.

In this society, there was no social, racial, political, or economic integration. This was principally because Cuba was a Spanish colony and that the primary interest of the Spanish government was in holding its power through maintaining the polarized situation on the island; the more divided that Cuba was, the easier it was for the Spaniards to exploit its economic resources and to preserve their political power. For more than three centuries the Spanish authorities —in the same manner as the other European colonial powers in other lands—maintained this deplorable situation.

But despite the crushing influence of Spanish colonialism, new ideas found their way to Cuba. By the middle of the 19th century there were political tendencies in the following directions: national independence; reformism (with Cuba remaining a Spanish colony); integration into the United States; and integration into Spain. None of these currents was indigenous; they all came from abroad, because the creole intelligentsia was weak and saw itself and its country's situation as it was seen from abroad, be it in France, Spain, or the U.S.

At this time, the revolutionary independence tendency, even though it had taken root among the creoles, was still in an intellectual phase; it had not yet entered its conspiratorial stage. Cuban reformism was aimed at obtaining small economic and political changes in return for maintaining the status quo. This tendency had gained some influence among the sugar barons and the large and small creole bourgeois classes, in large part due to the obvious failure of integrationist efforts (in regard to the U.S.). For their part, those Cuban creoles living in the United States were largely in favor of Cuba's joining the U.S. (or at least its southern states) in the period before the U.S. Civil War. But the failure of two exile invasions of Cuba at the beginning of the 1850s (mounted with the help of southern secessionist elements) and the defeat of the South in the Civil War dampened, but did not extinguish, the hopes of Cuba's annexation by the United States.

Ultimately, the most influential tendency in the mid 19th century was that of integration with Spain. This was natural given that the most powerful classes in Cuba depended upon Spanish colonial power—both political and economic—to maintain their privileged positions. Their slogan made their position extremely clear: "Cuba española." At the same time, those Cubans outside of the favored social classes either didn't have—or didn't dare to express—social or political opinions.

Nonetheless, in the 1850s new social concepts began to spread among Cuban and Spanish workers at the bottom of the social pyramid. The massive Spanish emigration to Cuba around 1850, inspired by the fear of the creole ruling class and the Spanish crown of an "Africanized" Cuba, brought with it a series of totally new social concepts, to which the Spanish/Cuban proletariat was receptive. This isn't surprising given the miserable conditions of Cuba's workers at the time. Spanish immigrants were treated as virtual slaves by their own countrymen, and 16- or 18-hour work days, seven days a week, were typical. One important industry in which such conditions were common was tobacco, in which not only was the work unhealthy and the pay low, but the long work hours were filled with monotony in unsafe working conditions. So, the ideas that the newly arrived Spanish workers brought with them interacted with the misery of Cuban workers, slaves, and campesinos to produce a new Cuban social movement.

It was at this time that the social ideas of the French typographer, Pierre-Joseph Proudhon, one of the most original socialist thinkers of the 19th century, became influential in Cuba. Proudhon's economic theories and social ideas—often lumped together under the title "mutualism"—had a great impact in Europe, and decisively influenced the origins of Cuban anarchism. The French thinker had disciples among the progressive workers and artisans on the island, and especially among those in the tobacco industry—the first in which some sort of class consciousness developed among Cuban workers.

In 1857, the first Proudhonian mutualist society was founded in Cuba, with the intention of creating a workers' organization free of state and dominator-class influence. This was the first step toward the creation of a civil society within the Cuban proletariat, even though, unfortunately, as the Spanish historian Casanovas Codina notes, the artisans associations founded at this time were "racially segregated and restricted to artisans from the same neighborhood. But they laid the foundation from which Cuban organized labor would grow and evolve in the future."

In 1865, the first strike threat occurred in Cuba. It took place on August 14 at the Hija de Cabañas y Carbajal and El Fígaro tobacco works in Havana. The 400 workers taking part were demanding an increase in their daily wages, and the owners of both factories acceded to their demands.

At about this time the young Asturian, Saturnino Martínez, arrived in Cuba and went to work in the tobacco industry. He quickly became involved in the tobacco workers' associations and by the end of 1865 had founded the first workers' weekly paper in Havana, *La Aurora*, in which he outlined some of Proudhon's ideas, which the mechanical engineer, José de Jésus Márquez, had introduced to him. It was in *La Aurora*, not coincidentally, that Márquez proposed for the first time in Cuba the idea of cooperative societies.

Martínez, although influenced by Proudhon's ideas of federation and mutual aid, was not an anarchist, and his proposals regarding the organization of work in the tobacco industry, which he purported to represent, were not really revolutionary. His paper, *La Aurora*, even though in favor of workers' associations, saw its primary mission as that of education, that of helping the Cuban/Spanish workers develop intellectually. *La Aurora* defended the right of workers to free association, but this was the same position as that of the Partido Reformista, which indeed owned the press on which *La Aurora* was printed. Nonetheless, *La Aurora* was Cuba's first workers' newspaper, and Martínez took the first step toward the protection of workers' associations. He also initiated the practice of reading aloud in tobacco workshops, a practice which would have great utility in propagating anarchist ideas among tobacco workers in years to come.

Let there be no doubt about it: in the period before the Ten Years War for independence from Spain (1868–1878), the foundation of the first free societies and associations of tobacco workers, typographers, carpenters, day laborers and artisans lay in Proudhon's ideas and their influence in Cuba. The country and its workers' movement owe the creation of the first regional centers, secular schools, clinics, and workers' mutual aid associations—at the very least—to the French anarchist. The Ten Years War would halt this impulse toward social emancipation of the most oppressed classes, while at the same time it would ruin the creole sugar barons; and eventually this war would end in the enslavement of Cuba.

Those who participated in the Ten Years War—the first Cuban insurrection for independence—included tobacco workers and survivors of the Paris Commune who had escaped France, bringing with them more of Proudhon's influence. Among the leaders of the Cuban insurgents at this time, one finds Salvador Cisneros Betancourt and Vicente García, who embraced the Proudhonian concepts of federalism and decentralization.

But the first openly anarchist presence in Cuba cannot be discerned until the 1880s, when J.C. Campos, a Cuban typographer who had taken refuge in New York during the Ten Years War, initiated contact between Cuban and Spanish anarchists upon his return to Havana. The profusion of libertarian propaganda in the form of pamphlets and newspapers that arrived regularly and clandestinely from Barcelona, along with the migration of Spanish workers to Cuba, reinforced the transmission of these new ideas. As a result, a new wave of revolutionary, socialist Cuban workers proceeded to involve themselves in the Alianza Revolucionaria Socialista (ARS).

It was in these years, the 1880s, that anarchist thought acquired an unprecedented influence among workers and peasants in France, Italy, Russia, and, above all, Spain. Its principal proponent was the notable figure Mikhail Bakunin, the Russian writer and revolutionary who elaborated on Proudhon's ideas. The divisions between absolutist marxist socialism and revolutionary anarchist socialism had already been demonstrated in the congresses of The Hague and St. Imier,[2] as well as with the founding of the ARS in 1873, and the establishment of the International Social Democratic Alliance in the same year. Ideologically, the well known Declaration of Principles of the Social Democratic Alliance, edited by Bakunin himself, had established the differences between the authoritarian socialism espoused by Marx, and the libertarian socialism espoused by the anarchists.

The revolutionary concepts of Bakunin were adopted by the Federación Regional Española (FRE) in the Congress of Barcelona in 1881, and they had a definite impact on militant revolutionary workers in Cuba, supplanting the more gradualist ideas of Proudhon in the syndicalist (union) field. It was at this time that the Cuban working class began to achieve class consciousness in regard to ruling class abuses and began to clamor for social renovation and redistribution of wealth and power.

In 1882, Cuban anarchists began to struggle against the reformism preached within workers' associations by Saturnino Martínez, now in another phase of his long life; and this time his was a reformism more favorable to ruling class interests than to those of the working class. He basically advocated collaboration with capitalist interests to obtain mild reforms in exchange for labor peace, an approach which was forcefully rejected by Cuba's anarchists. Their combative approach

---

2. At Marx's behest, the majority at the 1872 Hague Congress of the International Workingmen's Association (IWA) expelled the leading anarchists Mikhail Bakunin and James Guillame, and placed final authority in the hands of its General Council, which Marx dominated. In response, the anarchist components of the Congress organized another conference at St. Imier, Switzerland, in which the French, Italian, Spanish, and Swiss delegations took part, as well as over 20 delegates from New York. While not breaking formally with the IWA, the St. Imier conferees agreed not to recognize the "authoritarian powers of the Council General," which made the rupture between the marxists and anarchists plain to all.

resonated with Cuba's working class, and it was at this time that Cuban anarchism began to distinguish itself and to gain adherents. One of its leading proponents, Enrique Roig San Martín, advocated that no guild or other working class organization should be tied to the "feet of capital." Under these watchwords, the Junta Central de Artesanos was founded in 1885 with the idea of organizing and uniting Cuba's workers in federations.[3]

Roig San Martín (1843–1889) was born in Havana and was without doubt not only the most persuasive and dedicated anarchist of his time, but probably the most influential and respected anarchist in Cuban history. This charismatic personality was a thinker and author whose writings first appeared in 1883 in *El Obrero* ("The Worker"), the first Cuban paper to espouse a specifically anarchist position to the Cuban working class. He next wrote for *El Boletín del Gremio de Obreros* ("Workers' Guild Bulletin") in 1884–1885, which was directed toward tobacco workers. And in 1887 he founded the influential Havana paper, *El Productor* ("The Producer"), whose first issue appeared on July 12.

El Productor quickly became "must reading" among the working class in Havana, and by 1888 was publishing twice per week. In addition to San Martín, other prominent Cuban anarchists worked on the paper; these included Enrique Messonier, Manuel Fuentes, and Enrique Creci. *El Productor* had influence beyond the tobacco industry, and in fact represented the aspirations of the Cuban working class as a whole; it was the first Cuban paper to outline the idea of class struggle, and it offered Cuba's workers anarchism as a clear alternative to Spanish colonialism and capitalism.

Alhough based in Havana, the paper had correspondents in Santiago de las Vegas, Guanabacoa, Tampa, and Key West. The material it published included locally written pieces, letters to the editor, and translations of articles from European anarchist papers, such as *Le Revolté*, edited by the anarchist writer/geographer Elisée Reclús in Paris, and *La Acracia* (somewhat loosely, "The Place Without Rule[rs]") in Barcelona. *El Productor* was financed at least in part by the baker Rafael García, whom the Cuban historian Rivero Muñiz calls "a fervent partisan of the anarchist ideal." The paper was circulated within tobacco factories, in other industrial work places by the workers in those industries, and by those who produced it.

The strikes that shook the Cuban tobacco industry at the end of

---

3. In this same year, the Círculo de Trabajadores de la Habana (Havana Workers' Circle) appeared, an entity that to outward appearances was a cultural and educational group, but which in practice adhered to anarchist ideas.

the decade were all organized by anarchists, and were inspired by *El Productor*, "the weekly consecrated to the defense of working class socioeconomic interests." The strike actions and the production of *El Productor* were backed by a committee in which many workers influenced by the ideas of the ARS participated. These included Pedro Merino, Francisco Domenech, Gervasio García Purón, Eduardo González Boves, Enrique Messonier and Enrique Creci. All of these were tobacco workers from various labor associations based in Havana.

In order to facilitate and coordinate the efforts of the various workers' groups and *El Productor*, a revolutionary organization with anarchist roots was created—the Alianza Obrera (Workers' Alliance). This Alliance, composed largely of the above-mentioned workers, provided the first test of the advocacy of an explicitly anarchist program among the Cuban working class. On October 1, 1887, following the foundation of the Alliance, and with the support of Roig San Martín in *El Productor*, the first Congreso Obrero de Cuba was celebrated in Havana, sponsored by another recently created workers' organization, La Federación de Trabajadores de Cuba (FTC—Federation of Cuban Workers), which shared the revolutionary socialist orientation of the Alliance. This was the first assembly of workers in Cuba in a form designed to enduringly pursue their social aspirations. A majority of the members of the FTC were tobacco workers (that is workers in Cuba's second largest industry), although members of many other trades participated—tailors, drivers, bakers, barrel makers, and stevedores among them.

The Congress issued a six-point "dictum": 1) opposition to "all vestiges of authority" in workers' organizations; 2) unity among workers' organizations through a "federative pact" along the lines of the FRE; 3) complete freedom of action among all cooperating groups; 4) mutual cooperation; 5) solidarity among all groups; and 6) the prohibition within the federation of all political and religious doctrines (which in the coming years would be the most-discussed point). The "dictum" ended by expressing "the principles of emancipation . . . [and] confraternity . . . of all producers who people the Earth."

Now more certain of an organization that would back them, the tobacco guild workers called more strikes in Havana. In October 1887, under the protective umbrella of the Federation, the Alliance, and *El Productor*, they called three strikes as a result of labor grievances. The first strike was called at the La Belinda factory; the second was called at the H. Hupmann factory, as a result of a worker being discharged without good reason and placed on an employers' blacklist; and the third was called at the La Intimidad (The Intimacy) factory. This last strike lasted through most of November, and according to Roig in a November 24 article in *El Productor* titled "We Will Rectify [Things]," the issues were "apparently" resolved.

In July 1888, the tobacco workers called another strike at the Henry Clay tobacco factory in Havana. The strike had been provoked by the factory's owner, Francisco González, who was president of the powerful Unión de Fabricantes (Manufacturers' Union), which was an association of tobacco industry owners. Roig San Martín was personally involved in this strike, and it quickly spread to other Havana tobacco factories. When it became apparent that the tobacco workers were in solidarity with the strikers, the owners resorted to an industry-wide lockout.

In these circumstances, Roig San Martín stated in an editorial on September 13 that rather than abandon the strike, out-of-work strikers should emigrate to Tampa, Key West, or Mérida (on the Yucatan Peninsula). This was a dangerous course, but with it Roig indicated that the Cuban working class could now defy both the Cuban capitalists and the Spanish colonial authorities.

The members of the Círculo de Trabajadores—another anarchist-oriented workers' organization, founded in Havana in 1885 and with a large headquarters that contained the offices of many workers' associations as well as a secular school for 500 poor children—met on September 26 and agreed to begin collecting donations to support the workers out in the streets because of the strikes/lockout. According to the American historian Gerald A. Poyo, they also sent three of their comrades, Fernando Royo, Eduardo González Boves, and Isidro Grau to Key West to solicit aid from the tobacco workers there.

Finally, in the October 18 issue of *El Productor,* Roig San Martín announced that "the [Manufacturers' Union] . . . has decided to enter into negotiations with the factory [workers'] commissions . . . [and that in this manner things will be] resolved in more than 100 factories." These negotiations resulted in an agreement that was a victory for the tobacco workers.

The organizing efforts among tobacco workers were not, however, confined to Havana. The Alianza Obrera was also well received in the U.S. centers of the tobacco industry, Key West and Tampa. In 1887, workers in Key West organized the Federación Local de Tabaqueros, which replaced a previous reformist association known as the Unión, and which embraced almost all of the tobacco workers of the city. The organizers were two outstanding anarchists, Enrique Messonier and Enrique Creci, who together with Enrique Roig San Martín constituted the anarchist trio called "the three Enriques." Roig San Martín was widely read among Cuban workers, and his writings had a major impact on the so-called Cuban social question; Messonier was an outstanding orator and organizer; and Creci was a man of action in addition to being a writer of some talent who grappled with the problems of labor and organization.

In Tampa as in Key West, the most important industry was the production of tobacco and cigarettes, and the labor organization remained in the hands of anarchists who had arrived from Cuba, or who traveled back and forth between the two lands. Some of the outstanding militant workers of this period were Carlos Baliño, Segura, Leal, Palomino and Ramón Rivero y Rivero, all of whom held anarchist beliefs.

In 1889, the workers called a general strike in Key West, this time with the support of Havana's workers. The emigration of workers from Havana during the previous year's strike, the voyages between Cuba and the U.S. by anarchist organizers such as Creci, Messonier, and Gonzalez Boves, the presence of anarchist workers such as Palomino and Guillermo Sorondo in Key West and Tampa, and the reading of *El Productor* in the tobacco workshops had created among the tobacco workers a consciousness favorable to the ideas advanced by Roig San Martín.

During all of 1889 minor strikes had broken out in various tobacco workplaces in the U.S., owing to abuses by the owners and salary demands by the workers. This labor unrest was appreciated in the Havana tobacco factories, and there was a feeling of solidarity on both sides of the Straits of Florida, thanks at least in part to La Alianza. By the middle of the year, tension was noticeable in worker-owner relations in Florida, and strikes had broken out in Tampa and Ybor City. These presaged the general strike in Key West.

The workers there had already founded the Federación Local de Tabaqueros de Cayo Hueso, and Rivero y Rivero journeyed to Havana to inform La Alianza about the possibility of a strike in Key West. So, when the general strike broke out there in October 1889, the tobacco workers were well prepared. The causes of the strike were working conditions, salary demands, and, in general, the enormous differences in living conditions between those who owned the factories and those who worked in them. Key West was entirely dependent upon the tobacco industry, and the strike called by the Federación Local with the support of La Alianza paralyzed the city.

The Cuban separatists (that is, those favoring national independence) exiled in Key West understood the danger to their cause posed by the anarchists and their strike, and came out on the side of the owners. This did nothing to add to their popularity. They falsely accused the anarchist organizers of the strike of being in the service of Spain, and they unleashed violent strike-breakers against the striking workers. Creci and Messonier were threatened, detained, and finally expelled from Key West by the local authorities, who were at the service of the factory owners.

For their part, a number of out-of-work strikers asked for transport to Havana, thus employing the mirror image of the tactic employed in the previous year's strike. The Spanish colonial authorities very opportunistically decided to "protect the interest of [their] subjects" and facilitated the exodus of workers from Key West to Havana. (This was opportunistic in that the independence movement was financed largely by Cuban business owners in Florida, and by helping the strikers the colonial authorities were dealing an economic blow to the "separatistas.")

Finally, at the beginning of 1890, despite the owners' use of strike-breakers and violence, and the expulsion of strike leaders, the strike ended with a triumph for Florida's tobacco workers. The owners came to an accord with the strike committee and acceded to demands for a pay increase.

In the midst of all this, the premature death of Roig San Martín on August 29, 1889 at age 46 from a diabetic coma a few days after being freed from jail by the Spanish colonial government, was a hard blow to Cuba's anarchists. He was mourned by workers throughout Cuba as well as those in Tampa, Key West, Mérida, and New Orleans, and according to the daily paper La Lucha ("The Struggle") more than 10,000 people attended his funeral rites. Thousands of floral wreaths were placed upon his tomb, and El Productor dedicated an extraordinary issue to him on September 5th, in which Roig's closest comrades and collaborators paid tribute to him. In his own words, Roig had always considered himself "a precursor" who knew that he would never receive "material recompense for [his] labors," but who was confident that his successors would achieve his goals "through the uninterrupted transmission of our [anarchist] doctrines."

Roig had little peace during his few years of notoriety. His defense of the workers, his social opinions, and his economic concepts caused him to come into conflict with almost everyone. El Partido Liberal Autonomista (PLA), which attempted to gain recruits in Cuba's labor movement, suffered the attacks of Roig; and his stinging denunciations of creole autonomism were famous.[4] At the same time, according to Roig, Spanish colonialism was the principal cause of the abuse and ignorance of the Cuban people, and he refused to stifle his attacks on the colonial government, an activity for which he ended up in jail. The specific cause was an incendiary article in *El Productor* titled "O pan o plomo" ("Either Bread or Lead").

As regards national separatism, with which one would logically think that he had an affinity—at least in the political if not the social sphere—Roig was bitterly opposed to it, and had little regard for the republican ideal. He declared that it would not be desirable if a Cuban workers' society were to follow the example of the Latin American republics and the United States, which he sarcastically termed "the model republic"; he believed that establishment of a Cuban republic would only continue the persecution of the working class begun under Spanish rule.

The clash between Roig's anarchist ideas and his opposition to separatism on the one hand, and the separatist ideas and antagonism toward anarchism of many separatist leaders on the other, divided Cuba into two sociopolitico spheres and weakened both in relation to Spain.

The marxist writers of our day attribute to Roig the crime of lacking sympathy for the separatist cause, and at the same time attempt to locate him in their ideological entourage, declaring in all seriousness that he was "in transition toward marxism." We can understand what this "transition" was when we realize that it consisted only of Roig's having read and cited Marx; like any other anarchist of his time (Bakunin, Reclus, Cafiero, et al.), he would have felt obligated to be informed about everything relating to socialism.

Roig is also accused by marxist sectarians of "national nihilism" and "apoliticism" among other heresies,[5] ignoring the many contributions he made: tirelessly organizing and advocating workers'

---

4. The Partido Liberal Autonomista (PLA) was the inheritor of the mantle of the reformists of the 1860s. It functioned as an electoral political party, and when Spain decided to have elections, its deputies represented Cuba in the Cortes (Spanish parliament). The PLA was a pragmatic party which fit into the liberal-conservative scheme of colonial Spain, and it represented the creole bourgeoisie. Its members were from the professional elite and were much more astute than the majority of Cuban politicians. It built friendly bridges to Cuba's anarchists in search of votes in the electoral politics in which it participated.

5. The term in the original text is "sambenito," for which there is not even a close English equivalent. It refers to an accusation of heresy read aloud in church by the Inquisition, and is very aptly applied in reference to defamatory charges made by ideologically driven authoritarians. —CB

struggles, general strikes, boycotts, etc., in both Havana and the United States, in defense of the most humble sectors of the working class at the close of the 19th century. This is an outright defamation, and is a good example of the marxist tendency to rewrite history under the cover of nationalism.

The actions of other Cuban anarchists of the time were also consistent with the ideas they held: they advocated and practiced keeping the Cuban labor movement uninvolved in electoral politics and government pacts, because they understood that the labor movement had nothing to gain from representatives of the state, whatever their political stripe.

During this stage of organization and struggle, the relations between the Cuban anarchists and the colonial authorities steadily worsened. The Spanish government tolerated union activities to a certain point, and as the anarchists had decided not to intervene in the island's politics and to stay on the margins of the separatist-colonial-autonomy debate, the authorities established a system of "vigilant tolerance." The anarchists took advantage of this, and also of the changing of military governors and their interpretation of the laws concerning workers' associations and the press. Captains general such as Manuel Salamanca were patient with the anarchists' activities, at least in the interregnums between the seizure of power by military governors.[6] This was the situation on April 20, 1890.

On that night, over a dozen workers assembled in Havana in a hall of the Círculo de Trabajadores (Circle of Workers) and decided to hold a demonstration on May Day, in accord with the decision of the Second International in Paris to mark the day honoring the Haymarket martyrs.[7] This proposed workers' commemoration would consist of "a public and peaceful demonstration," the purpose of which was that "the government, the upper classes, and the public in general . . . should know the aspirations of the working people." They then produced a manifesto making public this decision.[8]

On May 1, 1890, more than 3000 workers marched through the

---

6. According to the British historian Hugh Thomas, "General Salamanca attempted to bring in reforms but died mysteriously before he had been in office one year (1889). It was rumored that Salamanca was poisoned."

7. This refers to the anarchist labor organizers who were judicially murdered by the state of Illinois after being framed for an 1886 bombing in Haymarket Square in Chicago.

8. Those attending this included Cristóbal Fuente, Ramón C. Villamil, Eduard Pérez, José Fernández, Juan Tiradas, José Hernandez, Adolfo Horno, Melquíades Estrada, Federico Aguilar, Ángel Patiño, José F. Pérez, José R. Cobo, and Victorio Díaz.

streets of Havana to the stanzas of *The Marsellaise*, celebrating May Day for the first time in Cuba. Following the march, the anarchists held a meeting where 23 orators[9] spoke at the "filled to overflowing" Skating Ring hall, attacking the social, moral and economic conditions in Cuba, and demonstrating that there was now an active anarchist presence within the Cuban proletariat.

Following this public success, the members of the Círculo de Trabajadores inspired several strikes, and the social environment began to heat up rapidly. The Círculo began to include not only tobacco workers, but also workers from other trades such as firemen, carpenters, typographers, hotel and restaurant workers, etc. This is to say that for the first time almost all of the workers of Havana as well as workers from some interior parts of the island were organized on a federative basis. Of course it would be an exaggeration to claim that all of these workers' associations were composed of anarchists, but it's beyond doubt that their leading members and the agreements they made adhered to anarchist ideals.

Because of its worker orientation, we're also dealing here with the first steps toward what in the years to come would be known as anarcho-syndicalism. Havana at this time had a workers' organization of the first rank, clearly the equal of the Federación Regional Española. According to the well known Cuban historian, Moreno Fraginals, "The workers' movement in Havana was the most developed and the most class conscious in all of Latin America."

At this time, after the mysterious deaths of the Spanish commander, General Salamanca, and of a transitional colonial governor, another officer, Captain-General Camilo García Polavieja—known for his arbitrariness and despotic methods—took command of Cuba's colonial administration. At the same time, a wave of strikes persisted, social well-being continued to deteriorate, and a director of the tobacco section of the reformist Unión Obrera, Menéndez Areces, was stabbed to death. He had insulted and made charges against Roig San Martín, resulting in Roig's arrest and imprisonment. Menéndez Areces was also thought to be a police informer.

The colonial authorities evidently thought that the only beneficiaries of Menéndez' death were the Círculo anarchists—or at least

---

9. The liberal periodical *La Lucha* ("The Struggle") listed the speakers as Sandalio Romaelle, Cristóbal Fuente, Juan Tiradas, Prendes, Victoriano Díaz, Ramón, Villamil, Enrique Messonier, Pablo Guerra, Manuel M. Miranda, Enrique Creci. Anselmo Álvarez, Eduardo González Boves, Eduardo Rey García, Velarmino, Gerardo Quintana, Ramón Otero, Adolfo Horno, Jenaro Hernández, José Joaquín Izaguirre, Ruiz, Francisco Vega, and the concluding speaker, Máximino Fernández.

they used his death as a convenient pretext—and they detained 11 workers who belonged to the Círculo, accusing them of Menéndez' murder. At the subsequent trial, the workers proved their innocence and were absolved of the crime. Not satisfied with this verdict, García Polavieja, in December 1890, ordered the shutdown of *El Productor*, bringing an end to the second stage of this Havana anarchist periodical.[10] The repression from the "Christian General" intensified, and shortly after the closing of *El Productor*, he also ordered the shutdown of the Alianza Obrera, and prohibited its activities.

These persecutions on the part of the Captain-General, perhaps made because he had little sympathy for anarchists, perhaps because of orders from the Overseas Ministry in Madrid, didn't intimidate Cuba's anarchists, who quickly submerged themselves in clandestine activities. For their part, Cuban and Spanish capitalists—manufacturers, industrialists, and merchants—were enriched more and more every day by the sweat of Cuban workers, who were treated almost as badly as the black slaves of old.[11] These creole and Spanish capitalists feared workers' organizations such as the Alianza Obrera, and hated Cuba's anarchists with a passion. They used their influence to create reformist workers' organizations, and to pressure the government in Madrid to repress the activities of revolutionary workers' organizations in Cuba, the same as in Spain.[12]

Under these conditions, and with a good dose of secrecy during the celebration of May Day in 1891, Cuba's anarchists agreed to convene a congress in early 1892, which met in January after García Polavieja was no longer Captain-General, and the authorities were showing a more tolerant attitude toward the anarchists.

The Congreso Regional Cubano met from January 15 to January

10. The first stage of *El Productor* lasted from its founding by Roig San Martín on July 12, 1887 to his death on August 29, 1889. The second stage began with Roig's death and ended with the paper's temporary closure by the colonial authorities in 1891; during this time Alvaro Aenlle was the editor. The third stage began with the reopening of the paper in Guanabacoa under the editorship of Enrique Creci in 1891, and ended with its final closing by the colonial authorities in 1893.

11. Spain freed those slaves who fought in the Ten Years War (1868–1878) and formally abolished slavery in Cuba in 1886, the same year in which it was abolished in the only other country still practicing it, Brazil. As did former U.S. slaves, the Afrocubanos suffered severe discrimination for many years after being freed. Cuba's anarchists, in their congresses of 1887 and 1892, approved the entry of the Afrocubanos into their organizations.

12. A similar scenario would play out in the United States in coming years, with the ascendence of the (barely) reformist American Federation of Labor (AFL) and the suppression of the revolutionary syndicalist Industrial Workers of the World. —CB

19, 1892, and was met with jubilation. It didn't use the word "national," not only because Cuba was still considered a region of Spain, but also because anarchists had by this time repudiated the concept of nationalism. Seventy-four workers met in this assembly; it included delegates from all of the workers' associations and trades that existed in Cuba. The Congress's accords—after passionate discussion—included the words, " the working class will not emancipate itself until it embraces the ideas of revolutionary socialism," which in these years meant the ideas of anarchism. The Congress also declared that its members felt themselves "tied to all the oppressed of the Earth" and in "sympathy . . . with every step toward liberty."

Finally, in reference to the latent political problem existing among the island's advocates of integration with Spain, autonomy, or independence, the second clause of the Congress's manifesto states:

> The working masses of Cuba will not and can not come to be an obstacle to the triumph of the people's aspirations for emancipation, because it would be absurd that a person who aspires to individual liberty would oppose the collective liberty of a people, even though the collective liberty desired is that of emancipation from the tutelage of another people.

It's necessary to note that in this paragraph, which is without doubt the key to the future relationship between Cuba's anarchists and separatists, the anarchists established the difference between social liberty and political emancipation. Liberation from foreign rule had been contemplated by the independence movements since the first days of the 19th century, and would still be some decades in coming. Independence advocates had made what was effectively the unilateral decision to put breaking with Spain above all else, putting into the enterprise their will, power, riches, families, and even life itself in order to create a Cuban republic. The Cuban anarchists, for their part, understood that social liberty was more important than the republic proposed by the independence movement, and that a republic would bring little or no benefit to the workers, as Roig had argued. Nevertheless, in the 1892 Congress the anarchists declared that they couldn't oppose the independence aspirations of so many Cubans.

The independence temptation had gained many recruits among Cuban workers on the island, and above all in the emigrant enclaves of Key West and Tampa. The social conflicts and the strikes which had taken place in the previous decade had created a crisis between the tobacco-industry anarchists on the one hand, and the factory owners, bosses, and various capitalists on the other. The most notorious independence advocates had made common cause with the capitalists for simple economic reasons—their ability to contribute economically to the independence movement. In this manner, the ground shifted. Now there was a dangerous split between worker-oriented anarchists and independence advocates taking money from tobacco capitalism. The social question (i.e., workers' rights, welfare, and control of work) had been dramatically displaced by the political question (i.e., the matter of who controls the state apparatus).

The situation, however, began to change rapidly in the first years of the 1890s. The manifesto of the Congress of 1892 is evidence that Cuba's anarchists were inclined to reach an accord with the separatists, and thus cease being used by the Spaniards as a divisive element in combat against the separatists. This shift in position did not, of course, imply the renunciation of the anarchists' revolutionary cause. Nonetheless, the second clause of the manifesto unleashed a bitter polemic among the anarchists that would endure for years, between those who favored first achieving independence and then pursuing anarchist goals, and those who looked upon the independence movement as a worse-than-useless waste of time for working people

The response of the Spanish authorities to the Congress of 1892 was the prohibition of free assembly, the seizure and temporary closing of *El Productor*, the prohibition of workers' meetings, and the persecution of the Círculo de Trabajadores and the Junta Central de Trabajadores (formerly the Junta Central de Artesanos). Almost all of the organizers of the Congress were jailed and some were exiled, obliging the anarchists to return to clandestine activities. In the words of the orthodox marxist writer, Aleida Plasencia: "At the beginning of 1892, the workers were persecuted, more for their class-conscious activities than for their independence activities." This statement reflects the true nature of things at the time, and also underlines the surprise and violent reaction of the colonial authorities when they realized the contents of the *Manifiesto del Congreso de '92*.

The Cubans preparing for the independence struggle operated primarily from the coast of Florida, mainly from Tampa and Key West—working class focal points, which for years housed the highest numbers of Cubans in exile. These Cubans organized themselves into unions, and these cities were enclaves of patriots, anarchists, separatists, and enemies of Spain in general. It was precisely in these years of the early 1890s that Jose Martí, the most notable Cuban patriot of the time, recruited adherents to the idea of creating unified primary principles first, and armed struggle later, among the different separatist groups exiled in the United States.

At the same time, the Cuban and Spanish workers in the different branches of the tobacco industry contemplated the Cuban question from a social or internationalist point of view. Martí, with his eloquent speech, directed his words toward these workers with the idea of making them see the social advantages that would come with his dreamed-of republic. In contrast to Roig San Martín's fears of a republic full of bloodshed and hate, Martí promised them a republic filled with the sense of liberty and social justice, "with everyone included, and for the good of everyone."

Influenced by the persuasive oratory of Martí, the majority of exiled anarchists began to support the independence cause. This was affirmed years later by the anarchist Pedro Esteve in his *Memoria de la Conferencia Anarquista Internacional*: "Our ideals were accepted" by the anarchists who publicly backed the independence movement, but unfortunately they were not realized in this particular area. "In these anarchists one discovered that the patriotic fire was not extinguished. Below the ashes there were hot coals . . . and blowing on the ashes revived the coals, turning them into a devastating flame." These words of Esteve couldn't have been more correct; and it was precisely the oratory of Martí that blew on the ashes and produced the separatist conflagration.

Martí managed to decisively influence many notable anarchists, such as Creci, Messonier, Rivero y Rivero, and Baliño, all of whom came to accept his revolutionary theses. The majority of them, however, continued to hold to the ideas of political liberty and revolutionary anarchism, with the exceptions of Rivero y Rivero and Baliño, who fully crossed over to the simple independence camp. The support of these anarchist elements within the tobacco industry for the independence movement was immense, as much in the moral as the politico-economic sphere. Martí jubilantly received the *Manifiesto del Congreso de '92*, and at almost the same time decided to found a "revolutionary" separatist party, composed primarily of tobacco workers inside and outside of Cuba, who were now able to reconcile their anarchist and separatist sentiments.

At its founding in the first months of 1892, the Partido Revolucionario Cubano (PRC), in which Martí served as a delegate, was composed of autonomous, decentralized, revolutionary clubs, with statutes and structures embodying direct democracy. (The PRC was similar in many ways to the later Partido Liberal Mexicano, founded by the Mexican anarchist and revolutionary, Ricardo Flores Magón.) This is to say that the PRC was not a typical electoral political party, but rather an overall revolutionary movement, a way to independence. The anarchists who grouped together under the separatist banner were mainly in two organizations, the first titled—with a certain amount of irony—Club Roig San Martín, and the second titled Fermín Salvochea, in honor of an Andalusian anarchist who was admired by Martí, and who was a great defender, from prison, of the Cuban cause.

In regard to the tactical alliance between anarchists and separatists during the war of 1895, it's necessary to clarify one point: Martí had some idiosyncratic ideas about anarchism. In regard to labor matters, he considered anarchist precepts appropriate and just, but at the same time he abhorred the violence created by the class struggle between workers and the propertied class, and he tended as well to mistakenly differentiate between European and Cuban anarchism. Martí possessed, in contrast to most of his separatist contemporaries, a strong social conscience. He deplored class disparities and was convinced that the future republic would be the impartial solution to social problems, "for the equitable benefit of all classes," without violent impositions from any party.

For their part, the anarchists in Cuba and in exile, allied or not allied to political separatism, had a social agenda different from that of Martí. With Roig San Martín's example before them, they aspired to operate more freely than under the Spanish straitjacket; and a republic would give them that space. In reality, neither separatism, nor the democratic virtues of Martí, nor the ideal of a just republican government, were in those years the focus of the anarchists' revolutionary agenda. What they aspired to and obstinately fought for inside a republican regime was the good of the Cuban proletariat. "More freedom of action and movement" in pursuit of workers' rights was the goal, and what good would a republic be if it didn't serve the interests of the workers? Thus Martí dreamed of a republic as an end in itself; the anarchists regarded it only as a means.

In 1893, according to Pedro Esteve, a "tame tyranny" existed in Cuba, that is to say, another period of calm, colonial government readjustment. The Havana anarchists evidently took advantage of this to regroup and to reopen, in mid May, the Círculo de Trabajadores in another location, changing its name to the Sociedad General de Trabajadores (SGT). That year, according to the Spanish historian, Casanovas Codina, the May Day commemoration took place "in exceptional conditions . . . It was celebrated with meetings in several cities and towns in the western part of the island."

During the depression of 1893, the actions of the industry owners in Key West provoked a very critical situation in which both the authorities and thugs in the pay of the owners carried out violent acts. The tobacco bosses, allied with the local authorities, formed an armed vigilante group, the Key West Rifles, for the purpose of intimidating the tobacco workers and forcing them to "obey the law." In this conflict, the anarchists and strikers had the support of the separatists, who delivered that support after observing the position of their enemy, the Spanish government.

The Spanish authorities in Cuba took advantage of this tense situation in Key West to weaken the nascent separatist movement in that city. With the idea of excising the anarchists from the separatist movement, the interim Captain-General, José Arderiuis, attempted to win the support of the Havana anarchists through bribes. This maneuver failed, and both Cuban and Spanish libertarian-oriented workers in Key West continued, at least for the time being, to be allied with José Martí's already-founded Partido Revolucionario Cubano (PRC), which took the side of the workers.

But the unemployed Cuban workers in Key West were in a lamentable state of misery, and many of them returned to Cuba. The conditions in Havana were no better than those in Key West, and the workers continued to live under horrible conditions despite their move to Cuba. The separatist movement had received monies collected from these workers, and with their return to Cuba and with the economic crash, its financial power waned considerably.

The massive unemployment in the tobacco industry didn't help the anarchists of the SGT (formerly the Círculo de Trabajadores), who were unable to devise a solution to the dilemma, and the SGT itself suffered under the terrible situation. However, in the words of Casanovas Codina, "The arrival in Cuba of the workers . . . doubtless contributed . . . to consciousness of the PRC campaign . . . to unchain the war [of independence]."

This economic destabilization had as a consequence the weakening of the social process in which the Cuban anarchists worked. Nevertheless, at the end of 1893 a strike at the La Rosa Española tobacco factory broke out in Key West over the contracting of workers brought from Cuba. The owners' response left little hope—they ordered the importation from Havana of 300 Spaniards to replace those workers who had called the strike.

A commission of owners was formed to journey to Havana to speak with Lieutenant-General Callejas, and also with "two young leaders of the SGT, . . . Sabino Muñiz and José González Aguirre," with the idea that they would recruit strikebreakers to work in Key West. Of course Muñiz and González refused this proposal. Eventually, though, strikebreakers were recruited; but the solidarity shown by the anarchists toward the strikers in Key West was manifest. Politically, the plan of the Spanish authorities, in collusion with the tobacco bosses, was to fractionalize the continuing debate between anarchists and separatists by adding the nationalist ingredient, Cubans vs. Spaniards.

The anarchists, who maintained their principles during this time by not accepting a pact with the owners' commission and the Spanish authorities, were the losers in this affair. The separatists, however, who favored drawing a line between Cubans and Spaniards, fared well. In Key West, while all of this was going on, the strike ended with a pay increase for the workers.[13] The strikebreakers received a hostile reception from club-bearing separatists and anarchists—united for the first time in a social struggle for workers' rights.

The disturbances in Key West had repercussions in Washington through the efforts of Horatio Rubens, the PRC attorney following instructions from José Martí, who persuaded the American authorities to prohibit the contracting of foreign workers via Cuba. So while the anarchists in Havana suffered a temporary setback, those in Key West benefitted from this situation.

Given the weakness of the SGT, it was easy for the authorities to prohibit the commemoration of May Day in 1894. Pedro Esteve relates that at about this time he visited Havana for three months, during which time he published a weekly of short duration titled *Archivo Social,* and that he also interviewed Creci, before returning to Paterson, New Jersey to work at *El Despertar* ("The Awakening"). Esteve, who saw war coming to Cuba, felt no sympathy for the independence movement, despite his friendship with Creci; he thought, like Roig San Martín, that a separatist war would benefit no one, and he would oppose the participation of anarchists in the coming independence battle on either side—separatist or colonial. Esteve favored, rather, an attitude of apolitical neutrality.

In February 1895 the Cuban war of independence instigated by Martí broke out, and the anarchists who had rallied to his cause found themselves converted to combatants. Among these, Enrique Creci, who was living at the time in Tampa, stands out. In 1895 he founded the paper *El Esclavo* ("The Slave"), advocating the independence of Cuba from Spain, and debating the matter with Esteve in Paterson and with Cristóbal Fuente in Havana. Creci returned to Cuba in 1896, and died in a field hospital in Matanzas from machete wounds suffered in combat with Spanish troops.

---

13. Generally, the tobacco strikes at this time involved wages, but other reasons for strikes existed, especially working conditions, workers' rights, and black lists.

Messonier, for his part, was finally expelled from Cuba in 1893 after making a speech in the Payret Theater in favor of independence. After his expulsion, he played the double role of anarcho-separatist, and debated the matter of independence with the rest of the anarchist world.

To the misfortune of all, the social changes promised by Martí died with him when he met a premature death at the hands of Spanish troops on May 19, 1895, only 44 days after the war began.

Throughout this war period (1895–1898), Cuban anarchists both at home and abroad tended to act more in accord with their principles than with their nationality. While in Tampa and Key West anarchists such as Creci, Messonier, and Miranda were in favor of the insurrection, in Havana one heard opinions now in favor of independence, now in favor of anti-war neutrality. While Cuban anarchists in the United States tended to rally to the separatist flag, or at least to contribute economically to it, in Havana many anarchists were of the opinion that the calamity of a civil war should be opposed on principle, and that such a war would make their task no easier.

At the same time, the differences that existed in the anarchist camp during the war were not totally divisive, especially in Cuba where, despite their opinions about the war, many anarchists actively cooperated with the separatists. For example, the arrival of Valeriano Weyler—the new captain-general of the island, and a man noted for his lack of scruples and abundant cruelty—was met with an unfortunately unsuccessful dynamite attack on his life at his headquarters. The attack was carried out by three anarchists and one separatist who came from Key West.

In Havana, leaflets circulated urging Spanish troops posted to Cuba and Cuban colonial volunteers to desert their posts and cross over to the insurrectionary side. There were also dynamite attacks "in various places in Havana . . . such as bridges and gas lines," according to Casanovas, who imputed such acts to the anarchists. Retribution was not long in coming. Weyler "sternly repressed the labor movement; he prohibited readings in tobacco workshops, closed the SGT, and deported many anarchists."

Even though, according to Casanovas, "The contribution of the workers' movement to the separatists cause was enormous," it wasn't universal. Many anarchists opposed the war on principle, and believed that in no way would it ease the way to their goal of social liberty. They thought, as did Roig San Martín, that having a republic in Cuba would not change the social situation, holding up as examples the other republics in the Americas.

From Alaska to Patagonia anarchists were pursued with the same zeal as they were in Spain. So, as was to be expected, anti-separatist-war sentiments aroused bitter discussions among anarchists of the time; and despite accusations, the anti-war anarchists felt themselves in no way to be allies of Spain.

To the violence unleashed by the separatist rebellion, the Spanish government of Cánovas del Castillo responded with its customary violence without quarter, violence so criminal and repressive that it had little parallel in the Americas. Weyler had been sent with the categorical order to end the rebellion using any means necessary. A part of those means, the "Reconcentration Decree," caused more casualties among Cuban campesinos than did Spanish bullets. Hunger and disease liquidated in less than three years almost an entire generation of Cubans, claiming more than 300,000 victims.

This atrocity was intellectually authored in 1896 by the Catholic curate Juan Bautista Casas, the Governor of the Diocese of Havana. In the summer of that year, and under official ecclesiastical approval, his work, *La guerra separatista en Cuba, sus causas, medios de terminarla y evitar otras* ("The Separatist War in Cuba, Its Causes, Means of Ending It and Avoiding Others"), was published in Madrid. In his essay, Bautista advocated a strategy similar to the American "strategic hamlet" program in Viet Nam—"the concentration of campesinos" in order that they be unable to aid the rebels. Bautista proposed that "our forces destroy and obliterate all of the hovels."

Following Bautista's proposal, Captain-General Weyler, under the direct orders of the Spanish premier, Cánovas, ordered that all of Cuba's campesinos concentrate themselves in the nearest towns and cities, under pain of being shot, and a portion of the Spanish colonial army dedicated itself to dislodging Cuba's peasants from their homes. As was to be expected, all of Cuba's towns and cities were inundated by hungry campesinos with no means of earning a living. Neither Weyler nor the Spanish government had made any plans whatsoever to deal with this contingency, and multitudes died—not only among the campesinos, but also among the residents of the inundated urban areas.

Mortality reached figures unknown in Cuba for hundreds of years. The Spaniards had taken the war to Cuba's civilians. They ended their imperial rule in the same manner they had commenced it 400 years earlier, when they exterminated all of the island's indigenous people. The magnitude of the "Reconcentration Decree" genocide is aptly described by the British historian Hugh Thomas: "[Proportionally] it compares to Russia's losses in World War II, Serbia's in World War I, and [is] probably double the proportions in the Spanish or American civil wars."

The armed separatist movement responded to the Spanish-created horror with terror. By August 1897, there was a stalemate—the Cuban separatists had made no substantial progress, and Weyler had not pacified Cuba.

While the war lashed the Cuban countryside and the Spanish government was committing unprecedented genocide, the debate among Cuba's anarchists was coming to its end. Adrian del Valle (Palmiro de Lidia), a Catalonian anarchist who had known Pedro Esteve well in Barcelona, had moved to Cuba in 1895, from which he was promptly expelled to the United States. Reflecting upon this useless dispute, del Valle proposed a way out of the labyrinth of pro- and anti-insurrection disputes among the anarchists.

This was the first time that the matter had been discussed at an international level, and it wouldn't be the last time that anarchists debated whether or not to support "wars of national liberation." Del Valle reasoned that it was better not to acrimoniously oppose those compañeros who believed in the advantages of independence, deducing that the only beneficiaries of this polemic would be the Spanish authorities who had done so much damage to both Spanish and Cuban anarchists. In the end, del Valle successfully recommended a moratorium in the debate.

The cruelty of the war and its enormous consequences created great social tension in Spain, which in turn generated acid criticism of the Cánovas government by the Spanish anarchists. These sentiments were shared by those anarchists favoring Cuban independence such as Salvochea, Pedro Vallina, and the periodical *El Corsario* ("The Corsair"), published in La Coruña, Spain. From Paris, for his part, PRC representative Dr. Ramón Emeterio Betances helped to foment strikes and protests within Spain against the war in Cuba. For its part the Spanish federalism of Pi y Margall and Salmerón also advanced independence as the solution to the conflict.

As an example of the divided feelings of anarchists about the Cuban separatist war, in January 1896 the French Committee for a Free Cuba formed in Paris under the direction of Betances, and with the support of Charles Malato. This committee was composed principally of French anarchists such as Archille Steens, Eliseé Reclús, Eli Reclús, Louise Michelle, Léopold Lacour, Jean Grave, Sébastien Fauré, Paul Adam, and Malato. In contrast, Peter Kropotkin in London and Emma Goldman in the United States maintained attitudes of neutrality.

All of this was soon made academic by events in Spain and by the U.S. entry into the conflict. The principal and first cause of what came to be called "The Disaster" was the assassination of the Spanish chief of state, Antonio Cánovas, in Santa Águeda, Spain in August 1897 in response to the torture and murder of Spanish anarchists in the Montjuïch prison, and in response to the colonialist horrors being perpetrated in Cuba and in the Philippines. The disappearance of the principal author of Spanish foreign policy over the previous 20 years was the final blow to the already decadent Spanish empire. The execution of Cánovas, committed by Miguel Angiolillo in cooperation with Betances, changed the destiny of five countries. The elderly, incompetent successor to Cánovas, Práxedes Mateo Sagasta, advanced an equivocal politic toward Cuba, decreeing an autonomy that satisfied no one; it was too little and too late—demonstrating only the weakness of Spanish colonialism.

The U.S. government took advantage of this situation by launching a war against Spain in April 1898 and by almost immediately invading Cuba, the Philippines, and Puerto Rico; and almost as quickly the U.S. forced what had been imperial Spain to sign a peace accord in August of the same year. The war formally ended in the humiliation of the Spanish government with the signing of the Treaty of Paris in December 1898, which decreed the loss of all Spanish overseas territories. This was an unparalleled and well-deserved debacle.

The Treaty of Paris, under which Spain delivered its colonies to the mercies of the U.S. government and U.S. capitalism, at the same time guaranteed the protection of the properties, industries, banks, businesses and lands possessed by Spanish citizens in Cuba. Ironically, the Cuban independence movement, allied with the Yankees, had won the war, but had lost the peace. After 30 years of struggle for independence, Cuba shifted from the yoke of Spanish colonialism to that of Yankee imperialism.

2

Intervention & Republic

(1899–1933)

After the cessation of hostilities with Spain, the United States found itself as the undisputed dominant power in the Americas. Having concluded its expansion to the Pacific at the beginning of the 1890s, the eyes of the eagle, with its political and economic ambitions, turned to the Caribbean. Cuba represented, from the days of Columbus, the strategic keystone of the region, not only in North-South communications, but also as the doorway to the planned Panama Canal. The idea of possessing Cuba, be it through violent takeover or through purchase from Spain, had been contemplated for decades by the rulers on the Potomac. So, it wasn't strange that any excuse would do as justification for intervening in Cuba, and the inept Spanish government conveniently provided one.

There was, however, sympathy for Cuban independence among the American people. The segment of public opinion that opposed annexation of Cuba first caused vacillation, and later reflection, in the imperialist sector controlling U.S. foreign policy. This sector sought a solution that would be palatable to all parties involved in the Spanish-American War, and they managed to find one that appeared satisfactory.

The U.S. occupation of Cuba began on January 1, 1899. The military governor, John Brooke, complying with orders from President McKinley, and in line with the Treaty of Paris, pacified those who wanted integration with Spain—Weyler's former fanatics —with promises of an iron fist. He also offered posts in the new civil administration to both those who sought autonomy from Spain, but not formal independence, and those who had sought formal independence. He disarmed the army of Máximo Gomez in the same manner as the U.S. disarmed the Apaches—by paying for rifles. And he promised Cuba's businessmen and industrialists economic growth and "social peace."

The pro-independence patriots, who appeared to have lost the political battle—be it through political ineptitude or rapacity for power—had to content themselves with the promise of future independence. This promised independence was conditional upon their talent for governing, good conduct, and honest intentions during this period when they were put to the test. Of course, given that the government in Washington was ceding them the right to independence, it expected these domesticated separatists to play by its rules of the game.

Thus was the stage set during the first U.S. occupation of Cuba; and several things happened during it worthy of mention. The first symptom of social unrest occurred with the exhumation of the remains of Enrique Creci from an unmarked grave in Matanzas. Upon the transport of his body to Havana, a group of war-of-independence officers and veterans in the funeral cortege clashed with the newly created Cuban police after the police prohibited a worker armed with a red banner from marching in the procession. A melee broke out between the anarchists and veterans on one side, and the police on the other. As Antonio Penichet put it, "And so the blood flowed." The separatist leaders in the funeral procession included Salvador Cisneros Betancourt and Juan Gualberto Gómez. Dr. Francisco Federico Falco was stopped by police before he could speak, thus preventing the anarchist orator from presenting his eulogy to Creci.

Dr. Falco had arrived in Cuba from Italy at the end of the war. He followed in the steps of his compatriot, Orestes Ferrara, who, despite his initial affiliation with anarchism, had allied himself to the Cuban independence movement. Ferrara, who reached the rank of colonel, had been named interim civil governor of the province of Las Villas. He relates in his memoirs that a strike broke out against merchants, Spanish industrialists and the British-owned railroad company in Sagua la Grande. Ferrara sided with the workers. He states, "It was necessary to rescue Cuba through raising wages [because] the income of the capitalists had increased by 200%." Siding with the workers created problems for him with the occupying authorities, and he was forced to resign his post and leave Cuba temporarily. Dr. Falco followed him.

During this same year, 1899, a new stage of social struggle began in Cuba. Its first manifestation was the "Masons' Strike," which began on August 20. It later extended to the entire construction trade, and was organized and backed by Cuba's anarchists, who had regrouped into a new organization under the name Alianza de Trabajadores. In September, after a public meeting and publication of a manifesto in which the anarchists alluded to the "international struggle for the eight-hour day, the red flag of the workers, the Chicago martyrs," the police arrested the Alianza's principal organizers, Francisco de Armas, Serafin Busto, Juan Aller, Francisco Carballeda and Evaristo Estenoz (who was murdered in 1912 during the race war that broke out in Oriente province). The governor of Havana, William Lodlow, promised an adequate punishment for "the enemies of society who wave the red flag of anarchy." These "enemies" apparently included two new anarchist publications which backed the strike, ¡Tierra!, under the direction of Abelardo Saavedra, and the short-lived El Nuevo Ideal (1899–1901), under the direction of Adrián del Valle, who had returned from New York along with Luis Barcia and other compañeros with the idea of founding this new publication.

The strike ended with an apparent proletarian failure. The workers had never received the full backing of the public who, intimidated and coerced, had turned pessimistic. Strikes, they were assured by the authorities, endangered the future republic. Despite this reverse, two weeks after having ended the strike, the bricklayers received a raise and a promise to "study" their demand for an eight-hour day—a demand that was finally realized 34 years later.

In September 1899, a new, more moderate—but under notable libertarian influence—labor organization appeared, the Liga General de Trabajadores. Its organizers were Enrique Messonier, Ramón Rivero y Rivero, Ambrosio Borges and José Rivas. The League backed a new periodical directed by Messonier, ¡Alerta! This group of anarchists had returned from Tampa and Key West under the independence banner, and still had reservations about their old compañeros in Havana. It was for this reason that they decided to set up shop separately from the Alianza de Trabajadores.

Despite failures over the previous decades, the annexationist temptation reared its head again with the U.S. intervention in and occupation of Cuba. McKinley's idea of buying Cuba from Spain in 1898, before the Spanish-American War, as well as the outcome of that war and the attitude of some separatist leaders, gave the annexationists reason to return to Cuba, and gave the anarchists reason to worry. The occupation of Cuba by foreign troops, especially U.S. troops, would not facilitate the libertarians' plans for social change.

According to the American historian Kirwin R. Shaffer, El Nuevo Ideal published an article signed by Luis Barcia in which "Barcia attacked what appeared to be U.S. designs for annexing the island, urging readers to fight against such designs." Later, Barcia reminded the U.S. authorities of the crisis they had provoked in the Philippines by forgetting their promises of independence for that land, and by not recognizing the republic led by Emilio Aguinaldo. Barcia also reminded the Cuban separatists of their duty to struggle for total independence, and, according to Shaffer, "led the anarchist critique of the meaning of independence, challenging the elite's abandonment of the popular sentiment for broad social change."

In the same publication, Barcia insisted on concrete aid to the campesinos who still suffered in the cities as a result of the Reconcentration Decree. Shaffer notes: "Barcia claimed that 400,000 reconcentrados were slowly dying in the cities from starvation . . . Families should have been able to return to their lands . . . but the rich and the government appeared unconcerned." This demonstrated not only humanitarian concerns, but that Cuba's anarchists desired to build solidarity between urban workers and their rural cousins.

Meanwhile, Adrian del Valle opposed the creation of a workers party as proposed by Messonier, Rivero y Rivero, and even the *Memorándum Tipográfico* (organ of the typographical workers), reminding them of the agreements at the workers' congress of 1887 and the lessons learned from the independence struggle against Spain, in which neither the anarchists nor the separatists had taken part in colonial electoral politics.

In December, McKinley replaced John Brooke as military governor with Leonard Wood—who was hard-line and more authoritarian. And at the beginning of Wood's rule, Errico Malatesta arrived in Havana.

The Italian anarchist writer and thinker was one of the most advanced anarchist theoreticians of his time. As a resident of Paterson, New Jersey, Malatesta was also well known to the occupying authorities. His numerous talks in the Círculo de Trabajadores and also in the neighboring (to Havana) town of Regla were received by a wide audience that filled the halls. He was interviewed in several periodicals, where he advanced "the Idea," but he also suffered delays and temporary prohibitions of various speeches until the provincial government decided to suspend his right to address meetings, even though he had already been prohibited from mentioning the word "anarchy" in his discourses.

There was a final, definitive prohibition of Malatesta's talks and, on Malatesta's initiative, Adrián del Valle requested a meeting including Malatesta with the civil governor, Emilio Nuñez, who had mounted pro-independence military expeditions from the United States. Nuñez was well known to Cuban anarchists living in the U.S. He was also responsible for denying Malatesta the right to speak in public. In their meeting, Nuñez declared that, "a law exists from the time of Spanish rule that prohibits anarchist propaganda." According to del Valle, Malatesta responded, "With all due respect, one observes that when General Nuñez fought the Spanish government, it didn't bother him to disobey the Spanish laws that he's now so committed to upholding."

Even though Nuñez perceived the irony, he didn't appreciate it, and Malatesta left Cuba, still barred from speaking in public. Manuel M. Miranda, who, according to del Valle, had been "deported to Chafarinas [during the war], not for being an insurrectionist, but for being an anarchist," wrote several articles in the liberal periodical *La Discusión* "attacking the governor and those nationalist political elements" who had pressured Nuñez to make the arbitrary decision banning Malatesta's speeches. This was despite Malatesta's having favored Cuban independence. During the war of independence, del Valle recalls that Malatesta had maintained a constant, pro-independence attitude, and that he had stated, an "individual who struggles against tyranny of any type cannot help but struggle for the independence of Cuba." (This put Malatesta more in the camp of Messonier, Creci, and Miranda than that of Roig San Martín.)

Before returning to the United States, Malatesta wrote an article for *La Discusión*. In it, he expressed a "potent sympathy" for "these valiant Cuban workers, both black and white . . . who have welcomed me so cordially." He went on to say that he was sure that Cuba's anarchists would "take their place among the most advanced elements . . . struggling for the total emancipation of all humanity." Malatesta lamented the imposition "upon the Cuban people of the same Spanish laws" against which they had struggled, and that in that struggle "thousands of Cubans had died, including Martí, Maceo and Creci." Malatesta stated that the class struggle would not cease because of the declaration of a republic, and he reminded his compañeros that the social question continued to be as pertinent in the present as in Spanish colonial times, because the laws had not changed. The future republic, Malatesta hoped, would give the anarchists more room in which to act, but at the same time he predicted that the social panorama would continue to deteriorate.

As could be seen, the situation of Cuba's anarchists under the Yankee occupation government was the same that existed when Spain ruled the island, with the aggravating factors that the remnants of the pro-independence movement still appeared not to understand libertarian ideas and that the progressive ideology of the PRC had died with Martí. Cuba's anarchists faced a difficult task.

At the turn of the century, Cuba was still divided into a deeply polarized class system. On the one hand, there was a powerful minority that represented capital and foreign interests. This class was legitimized by the Constitution of 1901, and was supported by the government of the day; it was comprised of Cubans as much as Spaniards, and it included entrepreneurs, merchants, and industrialists. On the other hand, there was the great majority of the population—workers and campesinos submerged in poverty, attempting to escape hunger and to recover from the misery left in the wake of the war of extermination between Spain and the pro-independence movement.

The island was in a state of total prostration, and therefore it was very difficult—given their almost total lack of resources—for Cuba's anarchists to mount a social struggle under such deplorable conditions. But even under these conditions, the anarchists helped to organize many strikes, some of which were won, some of which were lost.

Before the inauguration of the dreamed-of republic, nascent U.S. imperialism imposed the Platt Amendment to the Cuban Constitution. Under it, as a complement to the Treaty of Paris, the U.S. government abrogated to itself the right to intervene in Cuba and the other former Spanish colonies any time its political or economic interests were threatened. The Platt Amendment was not only insulting but also onerous to the people of Cuba, because under it they would have to pay not only for U.S. military expeditions, but also for occupations and their concomitant bureaucracy.

The reason for the imposition of the Platt Amendment was, of course, to protect the already huge U.S. economic interests in the island; and if the Cuban republic failed or went in a direction not to the liking of U.S. interests, the Amendment would provide a convenient pretext for intervention in or annexation of the island. But despite the odious nature of the Platt Amendment, opposition to it was weak in the early years of the 20th century.

The anarchists were among the few to attack this abuse. Both *¡Tierra!* and *El Nuevo Ideal* published energetic protests against the Amendment. The reasons for this were clear. According to Shaffer, "From an anarchist perspective, it was obvious that Platt negated Cuba's independence." Later, del Valle would remind the Cubans of their spirit of rebellion by invoking the memory of Antonio Maceo, the most famous black general in Cuban history, who was one of the heroes of the war of independence and who, like Martí, died in battle. Del Valle declared that if Maceo could rise from the dead and see what was happening in Cuba, shame and indignation would kill him. It's rather ironic that this appeal came from an anarchist, who was by nature anti-nationalist. Yet this anarchist appealed to the memory of a Cuban hero to make this political point—a point which in reality should have been made by the former separatist leaders and their followers. But they were intent on "independence," whatever the price and however illusionary.

The people of Cuba received the advent of the First Republic, on May 20, 1902, with genuine jubilation—despite the insertion of the Platt Amendment into their constitution the previous year. The new president, Tomás Estrada Palma, had served as the PRC representative in New York, and was now an old man of 70. He felt little sympathy for the anarchists, despite the support they had given to the independence cause. The second man of importance in Cuban politics at this time was General Máximo Gómez, an elderly authoritarian who resisted any and all types of social reforms, and who, like Estrada, had little understanding of anarchist ideas.

On November 4, 1902, a work stoppage, which became known as the "Apprentice Strike," occurred in the tobacco industry. This strike resulted from discrimination in hiring in favor of Spaniards over Cubans, and was backed by the anarchists in the unions and in their periodicals. The strike extended to towns neighboring Havana, and involved clashes with police. The strike then spread to other industries and the violence escalated. Despite the sympathies of many patriots with ties to the anarchists, the government of Estrada Palma refused to negotiate, which resulted in violent clashes with the new repressive government force, the Rural Guard. Finally, when the hoped-for popular backing didn't materialize, the strike's leaders ended it. The Cuban spirit of liberty had converted itself into pessimism and conformity, into a fear that any type of social disturbance would cause the failure of the first attempt of the Cubans to govern themselves.

The failure of the Apprentice Strike was more a blow to the Liga General de Trabajadores, than to the more radical anarchists of the Círculo de Trabajadores. The Liga was more involved in the strike, and its leaders had tried to come to an accommodation with Estrada, expecting some backing from their old pro-independence allies. As we've seen, no accommodation was reached.

The fiasco of the Apprentice Strike forced the Liga's two principal leaders, Messonier and Rivero y Rivero, to retire from the field of labor struggles. Rivero y Rivero ended his days in the shadow of poverty, and Messonier threw himself into the political camp, in the

Partido Nacional Cubano first, and later in the Partido Liberal, without ever renouncing the ideas of his youth, even though he had put aside the proletarian cause.

In the campesino sector, the anarchists commenced at about this time to organize in the sugar industry. This was the first time in Cuba that such an effort had been made in the island's largest and richest industry. The response of the owners, in the Cruces area in the center of Cuba, was violent. Two leading workers, Casañas and Montero, were murdered, which provoked, of course, protests by *¡Tierra!* and *¡Alerta!* The crime remained unpunished. In 1903, there was an unsuccessful strike on May Day protesting these murders.

In the same year *El Nuevo Ideal* disappeared; but *¡Tierra!*—founded and directed in 1899 by Abelardo Saavedra, with Francisco González Sola as principal collaborator—remained. Of all the anarchist papers, magazines, bulletins, etc. that appeared in Cuba, *¡Tierra!* was outstanding for two reasons: it was a weekly paper which survived the ups and downs of Cuban anarchism at the beginning of the century, and it published an extraordinary number of issues; between 1899 and 1915 over 600 issues appeared. This happened despite severe repression. Saavedra was fined, jailed, and was finally deported to Spain in 1911. But despite all this, *¡Tierra!* continued to appear regularly, under the direction of Francisco González Sola and Antonio Ojeda, until 1915.

(*¡Tierra!* entered its second stage in 1924 under the direction of Jesús Iglesias, and published 42 issues in that year. It published the same number the following year, until it was shut down by the government. It appeared yet again under difficult circumstances and under the direction of Manuel Ferro in the summer of 1933, and over the next few months eight issues appeared. This notable newspaper focused on agrarian problems such as the establishment of agricultural cooperatives, the living conditions of the campesinos, and the organization of workers in the sugar industry.)

The second U.S. intervention in Cuba took place in 1906, owing to a political crisis sparked by Estrada Palma's desire to be reelected, and the consequent near outbreak of civil war between the government and the Partido Liberal. At the end of Estrada Palma's time in office, strikes broke out in Havana, Ciego de Ávila, and Santiago de Cuba involving railroad workers, tobacco workers, brick layers, and urban transport workers. The government found a solution favorable to the workers, who had demanded—in the "Money Strike"—pay in U.S. rather than Spanish currency in the absence of Cuban currency. Still, the social situation continued to deteriorate.

As was reported many years later, in 1956, by the anarchist periodical *Solidaridad Gastronómica,* "In 1907, the first national speaking tour [of anarchist orators] took place; it included the fiery speakers González Solá, Abelardo Saavedra, Vicente López, and Domingo Germinal. Marcelo Salinas recalls that the orators included Pedro Irazozqui and Isidoro Ruiz. He also recalls that, "When [the libertarian educator and founder of the 'free school'] Francisco Ferrer Guardia was tried and executed [on trumped-up charges] in Barcelona in 1909, the crime had repercussions in Cuba, and resulted in numerous public acts," which, as one would expect, were violently suppressed. These "public acts" consisted of street protests carried out by the anarchists involved in the non-religious schools in Cuba, which were operated along the principles outlined by Ferrer.

All in all, the social panorama in Cuba in the first decade of the 20th century couldn't have been more frustrating. The new president, José Miguel Gómez of the Partido Liberal, who had succeeded Estrada Palma, had been a general during the war with Spain. Under Gómez' rule, the situation of the workers and campesinos didn't change much despite the improving economic condition of the island and its sugar industry.

Politically, Cuba was divided into two camps at this time, liberals and conservatives, as Spain had been under Cánovas. Not that it made much difference who was in power. As in other countries, whichever side gained power—the "generals and doctors," as it was put during that epoch—lacked even the most minimal social conscience. The problems of the workers and campesinos were as remote from these politicians as was Siberia. They simply divided their countrymen into two groups: those who supported them and those who opposed them. Both considered the anarchists—anti-statists by principle—to be their sworn enemies. The only difference between the liberals and the conservatives was that when the liberals were in the opposition, their more progressive elements attempted to attract the support of the anarchists through small favors, such as help with legal defense or through the reduction of prison time, more with the aim of manipulating them and creating social problems for the government than through any genuine sympathy. For their part, the conservatives dedicated themselves to the simple persecution of anarchists.

The outbreak of the Mexican Revolution in 1910 had a serious impact on Cuba's workers and campesinos. The words of Ricardo Flores Magón and Práxedis Guerrero in the pages of the revolutionary newspaper, *Regeneración,* and the guns of Emiliano Zapata served as spurs to the consciences of Cuba's sugar workers. This was in part because Flores Magón had a standing relationship with the Cuban paper *¡Tierra!*, which had attacked the Mexican dictator Porfirio Diaz ceaselessly; this had won *¡Tierra's* editor, Abelardo Saavedra, criminal charges and a fine from the Cuban government.

On July 14, 1911, the liberal government of Gómez was faced with strikes by tobacco workers, teamsters, and bakers, with the open backing of *¡Tierra!* All of these strikes, despite having just demands, roundly failed. The new Governmental Secretary, Gerardo Machado, instituted repressive policies and deported many Spanish anarchists (including *¡Tierra's* longtime editor, Abelardo Saavedra, and strike organizers Antonio F. Vieytes and Francisco Peréz) as "undesirable foreigners," and at the same time jailed many Cuban anarchists. This government policy of deportation, consecrated in the "Decree Laws," would continue for more than 20 years.[1] This was protested to little avail by the working public and its organizations. The government's accompanying propaganda campaign consisted of calumny for the anarchists and an attempt to divide Cuba's workers into two groups: "pernicious foreign workers" and "submissive native workers."

In this same year, there was unrest in the sugar cane cultivation are centered around Manzanillo, in Oriente province. In February 1911, *¡Tierra!* denounced the abuses, including shootings, that the sugar workers were suffering, and a sugar workers strike broke out that continued into 1912.

In that year, the Cruces Congress, the first conference of Cuban rural workers and campesinos, took place. Kirwin Shaffer relates, "Since before the anarchist-led 1912 Cruces Congress, the central town of Cruces had been a center of anarchist activity." He continues, citing the marxist historian Olga Cabrera:

> By 1912 Cruces had become a center for sugar production. From 1910 until his expulsion in 1911, Abelardo Saavedra had been publishing his anarchist *¡Rebelión!* from Cruces. Saavedra organized a Workers' Center in Cruces in July 1911 in an attempt to disseminate propaganda and to strengthen the coalition between rural and urban areas. To this end the Cruces Congress opened in February 1912, seeking to create an island-wide labor federation, establish rationalist [non-religious] schools, push for a workplace accident law, push for an eight-hour day, abolish piecework and establish a minimum wage. [These were] clearly more than just "anarchist" goals, but broader

---

1. "Decree Laws" went into effect immediately upon declaration by Cuba's president, and were later submitted to parliamentary consideration. They were applied instantly to the anarchists in this strike situation.

working class concerns. While Saavedra was expelled in 1911, other anarchists, including Enriqueta Saavedra de Fernández and the well known female anarchist Emilia Rodriguez de Lipiz, helped with the conference's organization.

In 1913, General Mario García Menocal, who was even more authoritarian than Gómez, assumed the presidency and became Cuba's first dictator. In that same year, the organizing campaign among the campesinos in Cruces was renewed with the backing of the Federación Local de Villaclara, which covered the campesinos in that part of the island, including Sagua la Grande, Cienfuegos, and Caibarién. The Asociación de Tipógrafos (Typographers Association) also reinvigorated itself that year and continued publishing the organ of that old anarchist trade, *Memorándum Tipográfico*. This was not surprising. From the middle of the 19th century, Cuba's publication workers had had one of the most combative unions on the island. The typographers had given Cuba Enrique Creci and J.C. Campos. In this new epoch, some of the most outstanding figures from this trade were Alfredo López, Antonio Penichet, and Pablo Guerra. They led strikes in Santa Clara, and participated in violent acts in Camagüey (in which the government accused the editors of *¡Tierra!* of complicity). There's no doubt that the anarchists responded in kind to the violence visited upon them by the government. Their response included street disorders and armed attacks upon the police in urban areas and upon the Guardia Rural in the countryside, in addition to some bombings.

At the beginning of 1915, the government deported to Spain, in accord with the new, anti-anarchist laws, Juan Tenorio, Vicente Lípiz, and Román Delgado, all of whom were accused of promoting sugar worker strikes in Camagüey and Guantánamo, and of supporting demonstrations in Havana. *¡Tierra!* was seized and its publication suspended. The government seized its last issue, went through its offices, and suspended its publication indefinitely. This left the anarchists without a publication of their own, but their views continued to be published in like-minded periodicals, with the anarchists themselves doing the typography and printing.

For their part, the anarchists involved in the campesino campaign in Cruces published a document known as the *Manifiesto de Cruces*, which for its literary quality had considerable impact and served as an ode to anarchist combativity. It stated, "We sustain our cry with the force of our arms," and "to remain silent is to accept."

Fernando Iglesias signed the *Manifiesto*, which circulated widely among Cuba's sugar workers, and which outlined the right to rebel against the exploitation and abuse of landowners and capitalists—

including the *norteamericanos* and Spaniards who controlled the greater part of Cuba's sugar industry. Iglesias was arrested a few days after the *Manifiesto* was issued. Other signers of this document included Laureano Otero, Manuel López, José Lage, Benjamín Janeiros, Luis Meneses, Santos Garós, Miguel Ripoll, Francisco Baragoitia, Andrés Fuentes, Tomás Rayón and Francisco Ramos. Concretely, the *Manifiesto* demanded the eight-hour work day and a 25% wage increase.

The sugar industry could have easily afforded this, given that sugar prices on the world market rose during World War I above the level of the previous century. Instead, it chose repression. The government of García Menocal violently repressed all protests, using the Ejército Pretoriano (Pretorian Army) and the Guardia Rural to persecute, deport and murder anarchists. In Santiago de Cuba, the young anarchist Adolfo Pérez Rizo was murdered for simply challenging García Menocal verbally in the pages of *¡Tierra!*

In April 1917, one day after the United States, Cuba declared war on the Central Powers, a move which—given its domination by the U.S.—favorably affected sugar prices and the Cuban economy. The following period came to be known as the "Time of the Fat Cows." Having perhaps learned from Cuba's independence debacle, the Cuban anarchists decided to remain neutral, despite the urging of the influential anarchist, Peter Kropotkin, from London, to take the side of the allies. (This was in contrast to the "neutrality" he had urged upon Cuba's anarchists in 1897.) As a consequence of refusing to take sides, the Cuban anarchists were accused of being "Germanophiles."

In 1917, García Menocal, the conservative candidate, decided to take the presidential election through force of arms, and the liberals rose in armed revolt, initiating a dictatorial period in Cuba, with García at the helm the first few years. In this same year, the Centro Obrero (Workers' Center) was established in Havana at 2 Egido Street. It consisted of a meeting hall and offices in a poor barrio near the center of the city. The Centro Obrero quickly became the most notable anarchist center of its time, and strikes, boycotts, and many other activities throughout the country were planned within its walls. The anarchists did all this under the watchful eyes of the Cuban government and U.S. and Spanish economic interests, which considered protests of any type forerunners of civil war.

In 1918 and 1919 four general strikes broke out in Havana alone, and the repressive state was the target of several bombings. In response, the state jailed and condemned to death the leading anarchist organizers of the time, Marcelo Salinas, Antonio Penichet,

Alfredo López, Alejandro Barreiro, and Pablo Guerra. The first death in the dispute was that of the anarchist tailor, Robustiano Fernández, who died in a confrontation with the police in front of the Centro Obrero. Later, the police killed another anarchist, Luis Díaz Blanco, on the street. Blanco's killing detonated a series of violent acts that culminated at his funeral in a massive demonstration against the government.

The U.S.A., now involved in World War I, couldn't permit this type of disorder so near to its coasts. At the request of the U.S. embassy, Washington sent a flotilla including three cruisers to Havana in a show of force. According to the Cuban historian José Duarte Oropesa, the Cuban Secret Service also supplied Washington with a list of all of the unions on the island, as well as a list of their leaders.

Finally, the government suspended constitutional guarantees with the object of creating a climate of terror; it deported to Spain approximately 77 workers it characterized as an "anarcho-syndicalist mob"; it prohibited anarchist publications; and it closed the Centro Obrero. In this regard, little had changed since the times of Cánovas and Weyler.

A temporary calm settled over the country in 1920 owing to the stabilization of the price of sugar; this became known as the "Time of the Skinny Cows," because of the low price of sugar. Cuba's anarchists took advantage of this lull to stage a workers' congress that attacked the high cost of living and proposed a series of "immediate and transitory" economic measures to resolve the situation. The delegates agreed to the formation of the Confederación Nacional del Trabajo. They also proposed to form an organizing committee which would "study the opinions of all collectives." Finally, they sent a "fraternal salute to the brothers who in Russia have established the USSR."

Cuba's anarchists appeared to have no doubts that the October Revolution—in which Russia's anarchists had played a very visible part[2]—was good news for Cuba's workers. With the taking of power by the Soviets, it appeared that the dream of three generations of struggles against the injustices of capitalism and the state had reached its conclusion. The Cuban anarchists showed jubilation in their own actions during this period, in which a few social-democratic and marxist elements participated, following the anarchist banners. But in this early period, little news had arrived from Barcelona or New York about the persecution of Russia's anarchists under Lenin. So, it wasn't strange that the Cuban anarchist congress of 1920 in Havana

---

2. See *The Unknown Revolution*, by Voline (E.K. Eichenbaum) for details on anarchist participation in the Russian Revolution.

responded favorably to the Bolshevik government of Lenin and Trotsky—a response that was echoed throughout almost the entire proletarian world. This attitude would change very shortly.

After the congress of 1920, Cuba's workers pressed their demands with renewed force; this provoked the inevitable repressive response from the government. Bombings shook Havana, and May Day saw another general strike. Penichet and Salinas were again jailed, and in protest a bomb was set off in the Teatro Nacional during Enrico Caruso's performance of Aida. For this single appearance, the Italian tenor received $10,000—a huge sum equivalent to the annual wages of 15 or 20 Cuban workers. Penichet and Salinas were condemned to death, but were pardoned and released at the beginning of 1921 with the fall from power of the García Menocal government.

With the new "moderate" government of Alfredo Zayas in 1921, the most constructive phase of Cuban anarchism began. The seed planted by the anarchists at the end of the 1880s had blossomed into Roig San Martín's "tree of liberty" and began to bear fruit.

Anarchist periodicals proliferated. *¡Tierra!* entered a new phase and its editors began publishing books and pamphlets. Other periodicals began to appear regularly: *La Batalla* ("The Battle"), *Nuevos Rumbos* ("New Paths"), *Vía Libre* ("The Free Way"), *El Memorándum Tipográfico, Espártaco* ("Spartacus") and *Nuevo Luz* ("New Light"). Almost all of these periodicals were published in Havana, although there were also sporadic anarchist publications in Matanzas, Cienfuegos, Camagüey, and Santiago de Cuba. They were distributed by individuals in workplaces, shops, tobacco factories, etc. They were also distributed by mail, when their issues weren't seized by the government. There's no data on the press runs of these periodicals, though it seems likely that *Nueva Luz* and *El Memorándum Tipográfico* had circulations of several thousand.

Clearly a proletarian cultural renaissance was taking place, in which even the most humble trades had information sheets. Libertarian literary and scientific associations were founded, as were workers' centers and naturalists' clubs. Anarchist literature circulated throughout the entire island, and the work of anarchist organizers, writers, orators, unionists, and cultural workers was characterized by exuberance. The anarchists—with few economic means and without any outside aid—organized Cuba's workers, both in town and country, into a force without parallel in Cuban history, a force numbering 80,000 to 100,000 workers (out of a total population of about 2.9 million at this time).

A new generation of Cubans emerged in these years, in the midst of a society filled with colonial baggage, class and racial separations, authoritarian governments, and U.S. interference. This new generation promoted radical changes in the social and political structure, and commenced a struggle against both native and foreign injustices. In their work for social justice for the most downtrodden, they succeeded in making anarcho-syndicalist ideals those of most Cuban workers.

The man who carried upon his shoulders great responsibility for this achievement was Alfredo López. He was an anarchist—despite the marxist rewriting of Cuba's history—and was introduced to libertarian ideas by Pablo Guerra, a black worker in the same typographic trade as López and Antonio Penichet. An outstanding militant in his trade, López emerged as a prominent figure in the congress of 1920, and his unifying work within Cuba's workers' movement didn't end until his assassination in 1926. Like a great many other Cuban workers of his generation, López was profoundly anarcho-syndicalist. Through his writings, his concise oratory, his union actions, his pragmatic attitude, and the accords for which he was responsible, it's very difficult to situate him in any camp other than the anarchist. Lacking in sectarianism, his acts were intensely unifying, and he knew how to win over the marxist elements in Cuba's workers' struggle. He also integrated reformist elements into the proletarian struggle, a positive action for which he has received little credit.

The founding of the Federación Obrera de La Habana (FOH—Workers' Federation of Havana) in 1921, in which López was the glue that held it together, initiated an anarcho-syndicalist campaign in the workers' movement. The FOH was not formed exclusively of anarchist unions, even though they were the most numerous and libertarian ideas were the most popular in the organization. Pragmatism was the order of the day, with the idea being to unite all worker and campesino factions in a single organization, although this was opposed by some anarchists who wanted a purely anarcho-syndicalist organization modeled on the Confederación Nacional del Trabajo in Spain. But in the end, the unifying approach of Alfredo López was accepted. (This dispute has been seized upon by marxist commentators, who have fallaciously used it to claim that López wasn't an anarchist.)

In 1923, a reformist movement gained influence in the University of Havana. One of its leaders was Julio Antonio Mella. Alfredo López offered his aid, and managed to persuade Mella to work with other students in the recently founded Escuela Racionalista Nocturna

(Rationalist Night School), which served Cuba's workers in the tradition of the murdered Spanish libertarian educator, Francisco Ferrer. And at the end of this same year, the Universidad Popular José Martí was founded, with the aim of teaching current political and social ideas. The direct relation between the future founder of the Partido Comunista Cubano—Mella—and Alfredo López has given rise to a number of hypotheses about the influence of Mella upon López, when the influence was actually the opposite, as Mella would declare years later, when he called López "my teacher."

In 1924, and with the undeniable tolerance of President Alfredo Zayas, a number of strike movements appeared among railway workers and sugar workers. At this time, another anarcho-syndicalist of the first order began to distinguish himself—Enrique Varona, of Camagüey, who was active in the railway and sugar trades.

In February 1925, the second Congreso Nacional Obrero was celebrated in Cienfuegos, with over 100 delegates, representing 75 workers' organizations, in attendance.[3] The principal agreement reached was to hold a third congress in the city of Camagüey for the purpose of founding a national workers' confederation modeled on the FOH.

That third congress was held in August in that city, with 160 delegates in attendance. It created the Confederación Nacional Obrera de Cuba (CNOC), which united all of the unions, brotherhoods, guilds, and proletarian associations in Cuba—in all, 128 organizations with a membership of more than 200,000 workers.[4] This congress, in its structure, its accords, and its principles, was strongly influenced by anarcho-syndicalist ideas—ideas which predominated among its delegates.

In the Acts of the Congress creating the CNOC, the most important accords were "the total and collective refusal of electoral politics," the demand for the eight-hour day, the demand for the right to strike, and the unanimous desire not to bureaucratize the newly created organization. Juana María Acosta, of the Unión de Obreros de la Industria de Cigarrería ("Cigar Industry Workers

---

3. Those in attendance included Alfredo López, Antonio Penichet, David Antes, Carmelo García, Alejandro Barreiro, Rafael Serra, José Rivero Muñiz, Manuel Deza, Manuel Landrove, Carmelo García, José Villasus and Emilio Rodríguez.

4. Delegates to the congress included Alfredo López, Nicasio Trujillo, Pablo Guerra, Pascual Núñez, Bienvenido Rego, Nicanor Tomás, José M. Govín, Domingo Rosado, Florentino Pascual, Luis Trujeda, Paulino Diez, Venancio Rodríguez, Rafael Serra, Juana María Acosta, Margarito Iglesias, Antonio Penichet, Enrique Varona, Venancio Turón, Manuel Castillo and Miguel Contreras.

Union"), was elected provisional president of the CNOC—the first time in Cuban history that a woman was named to such a position—and she made the demand, "equal pay for equal work."

A few days after the conclusion of the congress, the Partido Comunista Cubano (PCC) was founded in Havana by militant marxists such as Julio Antonio Mella and ex-anarchists such as Carlos Baliño and Alejandro Barreiro, with the aid of the Third International, represented by Enrique Flores Magón—brother of the well known anarchist, Ricardo Flores Magón—who had come to Cuba from Mexico.[5]

The PCC's members became a disciplined, selfless minority who, even if they had originally followed anarchist banners, would in the future—obeying orders from the Comintern relayed through Mexico—undertake to first supplant and later to liquidate all vestiges of anarcho-syndicalism in Cuba, the ideology that for decades had been the driving force of the Cuban working class.

The electoral triumph in August 1925 of the Partido Liberal, whose *líder máximo* was Gerardo Machado, provoked a sudden crisis in the ranks of Cuban anarcho-syndicalism. The new president, Machado, quickly realized that the recently organized CNOC could either be a political collaborator or a political enemy. He had reason to hope for collaboration. Inside the CNOC, a reformist element existed, which acted in accord with the American Federation of Labor, the reactionary American labor federation presided over by Samuel Gompers. Machado managed to attract this reformist element within the CNOC with government posts, while the allies that the anarchists counted upon within the Partido Liberal made themselves invisible. For their part, the marxists—after a period of blatant political activity, in direct contradiction of the CNOC accords—laid low waiting for better times.

Commencing with repressive precepts, Machado's government arbitrarily closed the Sindicato de la Industria Fabril Industrial (Manufacturing Union), because it had struck, arrested its black anarchist leader, Margarito Iglesias, and deported several striking workers. In September there was another strike among sugar workers in Camagüey, and anarcho-syndicalist leader Enrique Varona was first jailed and later murdered. (Varona represented the Unión de Ferrocarriles del Norte [Northern Railway Union], which at the time

---

5. Unlike his brother Enrique, Ricardo Flores Magón, founder of the impossible sounding anarchist Partido Liberal Mexicano, remained true to his libertarian principles. Hounded to death by both the Mexican and U.S. governments, he died of medical neglect in Leavenworth in 1926.

represented sugar workers.) These repressive acts provoked strong protests, which, however, came to nothing.

Because of the persecution, the political situation had become more difficult for the anarchists. The government unleashed even more repression, focusing on the anarcho-syndicalists, because they were the best organized sector of the working class, and because they had leaders of the stature of López, Iglesias, et al. Under Machado, protests which other governments had tolerated or had repressed to some extent, became the pretext for murderous repression. After the murder of Varona, López publicly denounced the act as a government crime, and these denunciations were sent abroad. But there was no violence on the part of the unions. Strikes were prohibited under pain of jail or "disappearance," and a time of state terrorism began in Cuba.

In October 1925, Alfredo López was taken prisoner after a series of bombings in Havana undertaken by government agents provocateur. By December, the most active anarchists in Cuba were either in prison or had fled to Florida or the Yucatan. In sum, intimidation, provocation, and murder were the political weapons of Machado at the end of the year.

López and some other anarchists were released from prison in January 1926 and were "counseled" to put themselves at the service of the government. At a meeting, Machado's messenger boy, his Government Secretary, Rogerio Zayas Bazán, offered López a paid post in exchange for his cooperation. López refused, and continued his anarchist activities. He was detained again by the police, and this time threatened with death. He again refused to back down.

On May Day, a secret commemoration was held in the Centro Obrero in Havana, at which López denounced Machado's repressive acts, and urged Cuba's workers to resist. Finally, on July 20, 1926, López was kidnapped and "disappeared." (His remains were found seven years later, a few days after the fall of Machado.) With the deaths of Varona and López, Cuba's anarcho-syndicalists and workers had lost, at a crucial moment, their two most valiant leaders.

The repressive politics of Machado against the unions had no parallel in the history of the island. Never in colonial times, nor under the republic—including the reign of García Menocal—had Cuba's anarchists suffered such violent blows. While Machado was celebrated by the privileged classes as a "nationalist" in a society suffering considerable U.S. interference, his persecution of Cuba's anarchists was unremitting. In 1927, the CNOC suffered another crisis with the "disappearance" of Margarito Iglesias, the anarcho-syndicalist grandson of black slaves, and a leading member of the Sindicato Fabril. The marxists within the CNOC took advantage of this situation, and began to appropriate, on orders of the PCC, the positions formerly held by the deported, exiled, and murdered anarchists.

The response of radical anarchist elements to this violent repression was quick in coming. They founded militant groups such as Espártaco (Spartacus) and Los Solidarios (Those in Solidarity), and later the Federación de Grupos Anarquistas de Cuba (FGAC), and began, in alliance with university students and some politicians, a violent campaign against Machado, who had been "constitutionally" reelected to another six-year term. They engaged in street fighting against the government and also in several failed assassination attempts against Machado. Of course, they weren't the only ones doing such things. There were other armed opposition groups, such as the Directorio Estudiantil Revolucionario (Revolutionary Student Directorate) and the secret organization, ABC.

In 1930, a streetcar strike broke out that was backed by almost all of the unions. This strike became a general strike within 24 hours, and was the first of its kind in Cuba under a dictatorial regime. The anarchists actively backed this strike, while the anti-Machado capitalist press heaped praise on the PCC and interviewed its leaders. This may seem strange, but during the Great Depression not only the working class but also the bourgeois class opposed the dictatorship, given that they were being ruined economically. The price of sugar had fallen to practically nothing, and social and political ruin was coupled with economic disaster.

But the strike itself was a complete failure due to its poor planning by the CNOC, now in the hands of the PCC. The oral testimony of Casto Moscú, Manuel González, and Agustín Castro, who participated in the FGAC's clandestine struggle against Machado, and that of Eusebio Mujal, whose father was an anarchist baker in Guantanamo, are in agreement. Hugh Thomas quotes Mujal:

> The Communists were . . .preoccupied with the anarchists as much as with Machado. . . . Party policy was to destroy all members of CNOC who were not Communist, *even by betraying them to Machado's police.* Several Spanish anarchist leaders were murdered by Machado.

Despite the persecution by Machado's regime and the backstabbing by the PCC, the anarchists, even though underground, did not give up. Contrary to what has been stated by both the PCC and by right-wing reactionary historians, the surviving anarchists didn't flee to Spain; they didn't abandon their positions in the unions; they didn't go over to the Machado government; and they didn't betray the working class.

On July 28, 1933, another transportation strike broke out in Havana, and the city was paralyzed when the streetcar workers joined the strike. The crisis deepened when the anarchists in the FOH rallied to the transit workers' strike, and it became a general strike. The U.S. embassy sought a political solution to the crisis, but Machado clung desperately to power.

His dictatorship ended in August, when a number of political factions—including, prominently, the PCC, following orders from the Comintern—conspired with the U.S. embassy (the primary source of power in Cuba) to liquidate their old ally. On August 7, a rumor ran through Havana that Machado had resigned, and the people took to the streets to celebrate—where they were machine-gunned by Machado's thugs.

In a political maneuver that can only be categorized as insolent, the PCC, in the name of the remains of the CNOC, made a deal with Machado to end the general strike (as if they were the ones who had called it). The PCC thus fell into the trap of believing its own lies. The payoff for its perfidious act would be the recognition of the PCC and the CNOC by Machado's government. The ambition for power had totally blinded the PCC. (It had also participated in the electoral farce in 1932, which seated the representatives of the coalition that backed Machado.) Present day marxist writers attempt to excuse these acts as "the August error." In reality, it was more than an "error"; it was a betrayal of the working class and the people of Cuba.

The PCC then gave the order that the striking workers return to their jobs, and tried to enforce this decree with the help of Machado's secret police, the sinister "porra" ("bludgeon" or "club"), which was guilty of the murder of a number of workers. The PCC's maneuver didn't work, however, owing to the enraged response of the FOH anarchists and the rest of the opposition to the "strikebreakers." The situation remained fluid and volatile for several more days, and finally reached into the ranks of the armed forces, who had no desire to intervene in this revolutionary situation. Finally, on August 12, Machado was forced to flee because of a military coup backed by the U.S. embassy.

On August 28, the remains of López and Iglesias were exhumed from a shallow grave and reburied after being rendered homage by a vast throng. On that same day, the FGAC published a manifesto to the Cuban people denouncing the traitorous actions of the PCC and the armed attack the PCC had launched against the anarchists' offices on the previous day. The only remaining offices of the Cuban anarchists in 1933 were those of the FOH, from which the Spartacus group had operated clandestinely. The FGAC's actions became known to the Communists following the triumph of the strike they had tried to break. In the confusion of the first moments following the revolutionary triumph over Machado, the Communists had decided to deal with the most militant anarchist elements, and, accusing them of being "collaborators," attacked the anarcho-syndicalists at the FOH with gunfire. A battle ensued between the Communists and anarcho-syndicalists, in which one anarchist was killed, and several people were wounded on both sides. Finally, the army intervened to stop the bloodshed.

The manifesto denouncing this traitorous, murderous act, signed by the FGAC Comité de Relaciones, gave detailed information about the anti-worker activities of the PCC and how it had tried to cover itself legally in the shadow of the CNOC in its zeal for power. The precarious cooperative relationship between Cuba's anarchists and Communists, which had deteriorated with the disquieting news of the persecution of anarchists in the USSR, first under Lenin and then under Stalin, came to an end in the bloody summer of 1933.

3

Constitution & Revolution

(1934–1958)

Despite the triumph represented by Machado's overthrow, the situation after his fall was unfavorable to Cuba's anarchists. Their most dedicated leaders and activists had been victims of governmental murder or had been deported. As a result, when there was a coup d'etat on September 4, 1933 against the provisional government backed by the U.S. embassy, the anarchists were surprised and unprepared—in what could be called a "pre-organized" state.

The new "authentic" revolutionary government, as it called itself, was leftist with nationalist overtones. Its principal figures were Ramón Grau San Martín and Antonio Guiteras. It was tied to the military men who had carried out the coup—privates, corporals and sergeants from humble backgrounds, and with all manner of social ideas—whose leading figure was Fulgencio Batista. This new government, the first of its kind on the island, defied the U.S. embassy and enacted laws benefitting the public; it also removed the Platt Amendment from the Cuban Constitution.

As could have been expected, the provisional government lasted only about 100 days. Given its "nationalism without a nation," its removal of the Platt Amendment from the Cuban Constitution, its decree mandating state intervention in the yankee-owned electrical and telephone utilities, and its passage of an eight-hour workday law, its downfall was no surprise. Nonetheless, it managed to damage Cuba's anarchists by passing the "50% law," which forced owners to reserve at least half their jobs for Cubans. This forced many Spanish anarchists to leave the island and return to their homeland, where a tragic civil war would shortly take place.

Thus, Cuba's anarchists found themselves gravely weakened at a pivotal point in history, while at the same time the Communists manipulated the cause of the working class with success, despite the setback of the August "error." They violently attacked the anarchists physically, while at the same time attacking them verbally with gross calumnies. These tactics would bear fruit in the following year; and the Communists would repeat them with even greater success in 1960.

The Communists accused Cuba's libertarians of being "yankee agents," as well as "associating and allying with ex-Machadistas, bosses, and even fascist elements," which at the time found some sympathy in Cuba. But despite the great damage caused by Machado, the losses under the "50% law," and the incessant Communist attacks, Cuba's anarchists entered this new stage with a vigor and resistance that was astonishing. They increased their propaganda work among Cuba's youth, and a second generation of Cubans rallied to anarchist banners in the unions and other labor organizations.

At the end of 1933, with the aid of the U.S. embassy and the support of Cuba's bourgeoisie, the by-then colonel Batista became the "strong man" of Cuba. Searching for allies among the revolutionary opposition, some young anarchists affiliated themselves with the socialist organization Joven Cuba (Young Cuba), led by the revolutionary and archenemy of the Communists, Antonio Guiteras, who had now fallen from power.

Again, Cuba's anarchists and the Cuban working class faced repression. In March 1935, Batista defeated a general strike called and later aborted by the PCC. And soon the PCC would adopt Moscow's "popular front" line, ally itself with the government, and follow "the democratic paces of Colonel Batista."

Batista attempted to legitimize his dictatorship through the electoral process. He had no political backing beyond the police and armed forces, and this wasn't sufficient for political credibility. The PCC came to his rescue. It offered him a deal putting all of the machinery of Cuban and international Communism at his service, and it promised to deliver votes in the coming elections. Batista badly needed this electoral support.

For the anarchists, the political situation hadn't changed much. Since the fall of Machado the authorities had exercised an iron control over the labor activities of the anarcho-syndicalists. They vigorously censored the anarcho-syndicalist press, and destroyed materials coming from the exterior, with the curious exception of the magazine *Cultura Proletaria*—founded in the 1920s by the already elderly Pedro Esteve, and published in New York by a group of Spanish anarchist exiles including Frank González and Marcelino García—which at times published news of the persecution of Cuba's anarchists. According to Helio Nardo, a witness to the events of these years, "After the failure of the general strike of March 1935, we found ourselves under brutal repression ... Thousands of opponents [of the

Batista government] found themselves in jail. All of the towns . . . came to be under military control."

At the same time, according to Nardo, difficulties were arising between the previous generation and the younger generation of anarchists. He recalls, " . . . the impossibility of reaching an understanding with the older militants entrenched in 'grupismo' (FGAC)" —here Nardo refers to those anarchists who had survived Machado's repression, the "50% law," and the military authoritarianism of Batista's early days. This "led to the founding in Havana of the Juventud Libertaria de Cuba" (Libertarian Youth of Cuba). Nardo recalls that its founders included Gustavo López, Floreal Barreras, Luis Dulzaides, Miguel Rivas, Julio Ayón Morgan, Teodoro Fabel, Abelardo Barroso, Modesto Barbeito, José Fernández Martí, and one young anarchist with the curious name Gerardo Machado. He also recalls that the meetings of this group were "rigorously clandestine."

For his part, Luis Dulzaides recorded his youthful impressions decades later. He stated that he joined Juventud Libertaria through Fernández Martí, and that he came to know "the highest figures of militant Cuban anarchism." Domingo Díaz, a pharmacist from Arroyo Arenas, near Havana, recalls that he came to know Venancio Turón, an old railway worker and a founder of the CNOC, as well as "Rafael Serra, a black tobacco worker who remained as a relic of the heroic times of the libertarian proletariat," and finally, Marcelo Salinas, one of the most prominent Cuban intellectuals of his generation.

At the outbreak of the Spanish revolution and civil war in July 1936, Cuba's anarchists rallied to the defense of the Spanish revolutionaries, and to further their aims founded the Solidaridad Internacional Antifascista (SIA) in Havana, whose members worked zealously to send money and arms to their Spanish comrades in the Confederación Nacional del Trabajo/Federación Anarquista Ibérica (CNT/FAI). Considering the depressed economic situation in Cuba, the aid they sent to their Spanish comrades was considerable. It's also fitting to mention the direct participation of Cuba's anarchists in the military struggle against Spanish fascism. With some of their members forced to leave Cuba by the "50% law," entire mixed families of Cuban/Spanish anarchists fought in the ranks of the CNT/FAI, among them Abelardo Iglesias, Manuel de la Mata, and Cosme Paules. A number of Cuban anarchists also went directly to Spain to fight. These included Adolfo Camiño, Gustavo Malagamba, José Pendás, Humberto Monteagudo, Pedro Fajardo Boheras, Julio Constantino Cavarrocas, and many others.

With the defeat of the Spanish Republic in 1939, many of the surviving Cuban anarchists returned to Cuba, as did many Spanish anarchists who sailed from France and Spain with Cuban passports obtained with the help of libertarian elements with friends in the Cuban Ministry of State. At this time, Cuba's anarchists began to collect funds to aid ex-combatants in need; when these people arrived in Cuba, they received a generous welcome from their Cuban comrades. There were cases of arriving anarchists being detained by the immigration authorities, who were then released after Cuban anarchists intervened on their behalf. As Paulino Diez notes in his memoirs, Cuba served as a trampoline for Spanish anarchists in the diaspora—it was a jumping off point for them on their journeys to cities throughout the Americas, from Chicago to Buenos Aires.

At the end of the 1930s, Batista was a military man lacking a popular base. So he decided to create a political coalition with the help of the Partido Comunista Cubano. And the PCC entered into a pact with Batista. In exchange for its services and its support in the next presidential election, the PCC was handed the recently created Confederación de Trabajadores de Cuba (CTC—Cuban Confederation of Workers), which had been created by the government and by its electoral allies in the Comisiones Obreras (CO—Laborers' [or Workers'] Commissions). The CTC was designed to be the largest, most centralized labor organization in Cuba, one that would combine all existing social factions, including a dues-paying anarchist minority. One major difference between the CTC and the previous umbrella labor organization, the CNOC, was that the CNOC had been designed to be nonsectarian and non- (or anti-) political, while the CTC was designed from the start to be a tool in sectarian politics, and had been placed under the control of the PCC by Batista. Thus, for the first time in Cuba, there was a marriage of unionism and the state.

But there was at least one favorable development under Batista. The Constitution of 1940 marked the birth of a new republic. For the first time in Cuban history, a constitutional document considered the social problem, and its authors tried to correct the errors and omissions of the constitution of the First Republic. Notably, it rescinded the Platt Amendment, though U.S. political, social, economic, and cultural influence over Cuba would continue until 1960.

Modern and progressive, this Cuban Magna Carta was the work of two generations of Cubans. Members of all social classes and all spheres of life had contributed to it. It considered in minute detail all of the problems that had come and all that its authors thought would come—social, political, agrarian, and labor problems from the previous convulsive decades of Cuban history. The 1940 Constitution was intended as an instrument of social-democratic reform, and all that remained was to put it to the test by putting it into practice.

The surviving sectors of the revolutionary anarchist movement of the 1920–1940 period, now working in the SIA and the FGAC, reinforced by those Cuban militants and Spanish anarchists fleeing now-fascist Spain, agreed at the beginning of the decade to hold an assembly with the purpose of regrouping the libertarian forces inside a single organization. The guarantees of the 1940 Constitution permitted them to legally create an organization of this type, and it was thus that they agreed to dissolve the two principal Cuban anarchist organizations, the SIA and FGAC, and create a new, unified group, the Asociación Libertaria de Cuba (ALC), a sizable organization with a membership in the thousands.

Over 100 delegates—both Cubans and Spanish exiles—met at the small Mordazo ranch, home of Juan Nápoles and his compañera Maria, in the Palatino barrio on the outskirts of Havana. They chose Domingo Díaz as Secretary General and Abelardo Barroso as Organizational Secretary of the new group. They also agreed to aid the Spanish exiles who were constantly arriving on the island; to take responsibility for the continuation of the libertarian publication *Rumbos* ("Paths"), which had appeared sporadically during the final years of the 1930s; and to call the "Primer Congreso Nacional Libertario" in 1944.

The large number of *cenetistas* (members of the Spanish anarcho-syndicalist CNT) who arrived in Havana in the years following the Spanish civil war were attended to as well as was possible by their Cuban comrades. However, the generalized unemployment in Cuba in the early 1940s obliged the great majority of these compañeros to emigrate to countries such as Panama, Mexico, and Venezuela, which, of course, weakened the ALC. Nonetheless, the ALC published for some time a new propaganda organ called *Rumbos Nuevos* ("New Paths") under the editorship of Marcelo Salinas. Contributors included Domingo Alonso and Claudio Martínez. As well, the ALC did carry out its plan for the Primer Congreso Nacional Libertario in 1944. It was held at the Plasterers Union hall in Havana, was facilitated by Manuel Pis, of that union, and elected as Secretary General Gerardo Machado and as Organizational Secretary, once again, Abelardo Barroso.

During the early years of the 1940s, the ALC libertarians dedicated themselves to organizing in the labor field. Given their history of work in the Cuban labor movement—and their primary role in it until the middle of the 1920s—Cuba's anarchists still had a lot of popular backing, as well as a reputation for honor, combativeness, and sacrifice, all based on a long and clean revolutionary history. The ALC began creating teams of militants from the recently formed Juventudes Libertarias (JL), with the goal of regaining the ground lost to the Communists and reformists. They founded "action groups" among both students and workers through the JL. These were propaganda groups of high school students and young anarchist workers who dedicated themselves to distributing anarchist books, pamphlets, papers and magazines in schools and workplaces.

Meanwhile, the Constitution of 1940 had enshrined the eight-hour day, which had been decreed in 1933—thus one of the utopian visions from the pages of *El Productor* in 1888 was finally fulfilled. At the same time, the Constitution regulated the right to strike, but still recognized it as a right. This situation, and the political infiltration inside the CTC, obliged the anarcho-syndicalists within the CTC to create pressure groups, with the object of challenging the inertia, bureaucracy, and the frank collaboration of the PCC and CO with the Cuban government.

Batista had been elected president with the aid and backing of the PCC. For this the PCC received ministerial posts, money, means of propaganda, and state protection. In return, the PCC conferred upon Batista pompous titles such as "the messenger of prosperity," and put at his service not only the propagandistic services of the party, but also the CTC, controlled from the heights by PCC elements. They had in effect converted the CTC into a political work force while thriving in the shadow of state power—thus once again betraying the true origins and principles of syndicalism in Cuba. For this, the Cuban anarchists conferred upon them the title, "frente crapular" ("debauched front" or "evil front"—a reference to the Communist "popular front" ["frente popular"] strategy of the 1930s).

Ramón Grau San Martín, the candidate of the so-called Partido Revolucionario Cubano Auténtico (PRCA) which had arisen in 1933, won the election and assumed power in 1944. The people expected substantial change from the new, freely elected, social democratic government. However, Grau San Martín allowed the Communists to remain in their posts.

The only important change in the Cuban workers' situation occurred on May Day in 1947, at the start of the Cold War, when the Cuban government, under noticeable U.S. pressure, expelled the Communists from their posts in the CTC. This decision served as proof that despite the deletion of the Platt Amendment from the

Cuban Constitution, those who had removed it still folded under pressure from the U.S. State Department.

There was a libertarian renewal in these years. A number of small anarchist information and propaganda bulletins appeared in Havana under the auspices of the Federación de Juventudes Libertarias de Cuba (FJLC—Federation of Libertarian Youths of Cuba), and a monthly "bulletin of the sub-delegation of the CNT of Spain," under the direction of V. Velasco and C. Trigo also appeared. Both the FJLC and CNT publications listed their address as that of the ALC at Calle Jesús María 310, Havana.[1] As well, the government decision to purge the stalinist representatives inside the CTC left the door wide open for the anarcho-syndicalists. They took advantage of the free elections in the various trades that made up the CTC, and managed to elect several responsible compañeros to posts in prominent unions.

The prestige and well-earned reputation for honesty of Cuba's anarcho-syndicalists gave them effective control of several important unions, such as the transport workers, culinary workers, construction workers, and electric utility workers, and allowed them to form pressure groups inside almost all of the other unions that composed the CTC at the time. Cuban anarchists in the interior of the island also created the Asociaciones Campesinas at this time, for the purpose of organizing the poorest, landless campesinos. These efforts bore their greatest fruits in the province of Camagüey, the old libertarian bastion, and in the port of Nuevitas and the southern coffee zone in the province of Oriente in the Baracoa-Guantanamo mountain range, where for many years anarchists had founded and maintained free agricultural collectives.

In 1948, the Cuban anarchists held another national congress. It was well attended, with 155 delegates present. The pamphlet *Memorias del II Congreso Libertario* records that on, "February 21, at 9 p.m., and with a great crowd filling . . . the halls of the Federación Nacional de Plantas Eléctricas . . . at Paseo de Martí 615 . . . the Second National Libertarian Congress, convoked by the Libertarian Association of Cuba, commenced." The congress was opened by the words of the old

---

1. This rented space was the size of a normal apartment, with five rooms. One was used as a bookstore; a second as the office of the ALC; and a third as a kitchen and living quarters for Vicente Alea and his compañera Fe, who maintained the place in lieu of rent. The ALC headquarters was in a poor barrio called Jesús Maria near the train station and the port. Most of the people who lived in the area were manual laborers, tobacco workers, shop employees, etc., and the commercial establishments in the area were such things as grocers, dry goods stores, coffee shops, restaurants, and shoe stores.

friend of the Cuban libertarians, Agustín Souchy,[2] who in those years represented the AIT (Asociación Internacional de Trabajadores/International Workers Association, the anarcho-syndicalist international federation). Marcelo Salinas, Modesto Barbeito and Helio Nardo also spoke. The Congress held a plenary session the following day, with Rafael Sierra presiding, and with Vicente Alea acting as provisional secretary. It created four Work Commissions: Organization, under the leadership of Modesto Barbeito and Helio Nardo; Propaganda, under N. Suárez and Manuel González; Finance, under Manuel Castillo and Vicente Alea; and Other Matters, under Antonio Landrián and Suria Linsuaín.

The Second Congress closed on February 24 with a series of dictums, which were published later in the year as a pamphlet. The pamphlet contemplated the creation of a libertarian society in Cuba, and appealed to all economic, industrial, union and agricultural levels on the island. The passage of the years has shown how important to Cuban anarchism this document was. It sketched the situation in those uncertain years of Constitution and Republic with a sure hand; it attacked Cuban anarchism's perpetual enemy, the stalinist PCC; it outlined the danger of the Catholic Church's influence; it declared itself anticapitalist and, above all, anti-imperialist, attacking both the U.S. and the USSR as "foreign powers," thus appealing a bit to then-fashionable Cuban nationalism.

Among the ambitious points on which the delegates had reached agreement, and which covered almost all aspects of social and economic life in Cuba, was one that stated the necessity of having an effective and regularly appearing propaganda organ. They chose the gastronomic workers' monthly publication *Solidaridad Gastronómica*, which already existed, and the Congress agreed to make it the official organ of the ALC. It would have a long life in Cuban proletarian culture.

Solidaridad Gastronómica's first issue appeared on December 22, 1949, as a four-page newspaper printed on newsprint and priced at five centavos. It was billed as "the organ of orientation and combat."

---

2. Souchy, one of the founders of the Asociación Internacional de los Trabajadores in 1925, had participated in the Spanish Revolution (1936–1939) and had written an eyewitness account of the formation and function of anarchist farming communes titled *Among the Peasants of Aragon*. Souchy was well known to the Cuban anarchists, and in 1959, knowing that he was thinking of visiting the island, *Solidaridad* had published serially his essay, "Libertarian Socialism," as a means of clarifying concepts and also with the veiled hope that the concepts outlined would be realized in a new Cuban society.

Its staff included José M. Fuentes Candón as director, Domingo Alonso and Jorge Jorge as administrators, and Claudio Martínez, Casto Moscú, Juan R. Alvarez, José Rodriguez and Roberto Cabanellas as editors. It appeared monthly in this format until February 1951, when its size increased to six pages; in December 1954 its size increased again to eight pages, and it began to be printed on better paper. In July 1956 its size increased again to 12 pages—the size at which it would remain until its final issue in December 1960. One hundred twenty-five issues were printed in all, and its circulation was in the 1000–1500 copy range. Even though it was published by gastronomical workers and was the organ of their federation, it reached a broader audience and its writers included the most outstanding Cuban exponents of anarchist ideas. In addition to news and analysis, it contained a book section edited by Domingo Alonso, which dealt with books on various libertarian topics. *Solidaridad Gastronómica* was one of the last independent publications shut down by the Castro government.

Carlos Prío Socarrás assumed the Cuban presidency in 1948, and followed the same tolerant path as Grau in the social and labor fields. So, the anarchists were still free to organize and to propagate libertarian ideas. In 1949 the anarchists within the CTC, along with other sympathetic elements, tried and failed to create a new labor central, the Confederación General de Trabajadores (CGT). The idea was to create a workers' organization independent of the CTC and its political influence and electoral participation; this was very much in line with the traditional anarcho-syndicalist position (such as that of the CNOC) which totally rejects unions functioning as political instruments of the state. According to Helio Nardo, one of the survivors of the attempt to untie labor from the CTC, "The idea of creating a second labor central was the result of belief in a non-political/non-electoral syndicalism, [a project] on which I worked intensely along with Abelardo Iglesias and Modesto Barbeito." With the support of Ángel Cofiño, a representative of the electrical workers, and Vicente Rubiera from the telephone workers, the Comité Obrero Nacional Independiente (CONI) was formed. Nardo notes that it ". . . had a daily radio program on RHC Blue Chain," and that "for the broadcast we would write daily in the hall of the ALC." Despite all of the opposition to this new step toward syndicalism free of political pressure, "it came into being . . . with the name Confederación General de Trabajadores (CGT) . . . with its offices in the Calle Águila."

The Tercer (Third) Congreso Nacional Libertario was held on the

11th and 12th of March 1950. It's object was reorganization, to take orienting positions within Cuban unionism, and to attempt to point the Cuban workers' movement in a healthier direction. The Congress agreed "to struggle against the control of the workers movement by bureaucrats . . . politicians, cults, religionists, etc. . . . and to expound the true significance of syndicalism, which must be apolitical, revolutionary and federalist," in this manner combating the existing syndicalism which was "tyrannical, converted in fact into an agency of the state."

The Third Congress ended by calling upon workers to repudiate the CTC as an organization "supported by the stalinist and false workers' allies faction, without a trace of revolutionary ideas, spirit, or practice . . . [and] dominated by dictatorial political parties and a corrupt leadership." The Congress also dedicated itself "to actively working with the workers of the CGT, the only legitimate workers organization with syndicalist tendencies and the one most sensitive to the true needs of the workers."

It was unfortunate that the attempt to create another union central would fail totally. The idea of creating the CGT independent of the CTC—and therefore independent of government influence—ran into formidable obstacles thanks to reformist elements, Communists, and the government. President Prio was well aware of the dangers posed by a new workers confederation under strong anarchist influence, which could not be manipulated by his political party (PRCA), and as was to be expected, he unleashed a propaganda campaign against the CGT in both the Cuban communications media and in the officially approved unions with the aim of derailing the CGT initiative. Prío's excuse was opposition to "divisiveness" or "factionalism."

In these years, as a product of the Cold War, Prío, motivated by U.S. "suggestions" and by members of his own party, also acted against the Communists. He declared the Partido Socialista Popular (PSP—the Communists' electoral front) illegal, and closed its communications media. This caused the Cuban stalinists to search for a new alliance with their old friend, Fulgencio Batista.

The Cuban government's fear of Cuba's anarchists at this time was not totally unfounded. Already by the end of the 1940s, the anarchists had regained considerable influence within the Cuban labor movement at the grassroots level. There were anarchist militants scattered across almost the entire island in small groups, functioning at the local level. Anarchist propagandists were also present in every provincial capital in Cuba. Sam Dolgoff, in his book, *The Cuban Revolution: A Critical Appraisal*, notes: "their sympathizers and their influence was out of all proportion to the number of their members. Anarcho-syndicalist groups usually consisted of a few individuals, but larger numbers existed in many local and regional unions, as in other organizations." Some influential anarchists included Casto Moscú, Juan R. Álvarez, and Bartolo García in the Federación de Trabajadores Gastronómicos; Francisco Bretau and his brother Roberto in the Federación de Plantas Eléctricas; Santiago Cobo, as Organizational Secretary in the Federación Nacional Obrera de Transporte; and Abelardo Iglesias, the General Secretary of Havana Province in the Federación Nacional de los Trabajadores de la Construcción.

One should also note the appearance of a new anarchist-oriented periodical in April 1950 in Havana titled *Estudios: Mensuario de Cultura* ("Studies: Cultural Monthly"). This new periodical reached beyond the sloganeering style that had characterized many previous anarchist publications; *Estudios* had a modern look as well as modern content —its socio-cultural text was complemented by numerous photos and drawings and excellent typography. Those responsible for *Estudios* included its board of directors, Marcelo Salinas, Abelardo Iglesias, and Luis Dulzaides, its administrator, Santiago Velasco, and its publicity director, Roberto Bretau. It had a circulation of 1000 and was financed by the various unions. This large magazine of 52 pages derived much of its modern look from the drawings of the painter José Maria Mijares, which appeared in every issue, and its use of photography (including nudes—a true novelty at the time).

One other monthly anarchist periodical was also published in Cuba at this time, *El Libertario*, the organ of the ALC. This periodical had appeared sporadically in newspaper format since the 1940s, and was under the direction of Marcelo Salinas. Its irregular appearance was dictated by finances, and it, along with *Solidaridad Gastronómica*, was one of the last independent publications shut down by the Castro regime. It was a four-page newspaper priced at five centavos, and its contributors and collaborators included Rolando Piñera (its administrator), Manuel Gaona Sousa, Casto Moscú, Abelardo Iglesias, and from México, Silvia Mistral, and from Sweden, Agustín Souchy.

In March 1952, Batista carried out a coup d'etat. The Cuban people received the news with utter indifference, given the moral and administrative corruption of the Prío government. A call for a general strike failed totally, and the CTC, under Eusebio Mujal (general secretary of the CTC, and an ex-Communist and ex-Trotskyist who had belonged to the Comisiones Obreras) quickly came to terms with Batista, despite the opposition of the anarchists in the CTC to the imposition of military rule. As an excuse for his conduct, Mujal told union leaders that opposing Batista's coup would have meant the ousting of those who resisted it and their substitution by members of the PCC, backed by Batista's military. For their part, the Communists took advantage of the circumstances to penetrate the CTC bureaucracy, but were unable to regain their once-preponderant influence in the organization. For his part, Batista embraced the Communists as allies, but this time in silence. The Cold War was in full swing and he had to be careful about his stalinist political associates.

Another significant figure appeared in this period: Fidel Castro, a young, Jesuit-educated politician from a bourgeois background, who sought to fill the vacuum of oppositional power created by Batista's coup. On July 26, 1953, Castro and a group of revolutionaries carried out an attack on the Moncada Barracks in Santiago de Cuba, which ended in bloodshed and with many victims on both sides. Castro was taken prisoner and at his trial, in his defense plea, he outlined a "revolutionary" program that was anything but—it was simply reformist and basically social democratic. His primary object was to reestablish the Constitution of 1940, which Batista had violated by overthrowing Prío. The trial concluded at the end of 1953 with Castro being condemned to 15 years in prison, along with a number of his comrades. He took advantage of the occasion by founding the 26th of July Movement (M26J). After being imprisoned for a few months, Castro was released because of a governmental amnesty, and he left for Mexico.

By this time the opposition to Batista had turned violent, and Batista, as was to be expected, responded brutally to provocations. The political climate was heating up, and the opposition, which embraced non-Castro as well as pro-Castro factions, grew rapidly. Preoccupied by the political situation, in March 1955 the recently named ALC National Council called for a National Libertarian Conference, which was held on April 24th of the same year at an ecological preserve in the town Campo Florido, on the outskirts of Havana. The conference had an agenda of 10 points, the most important of which was National Affairs.

Its report evaluated all of anarchist activities carried out since the Third Congress. It noted that one event was the closing of *El Libertario* in April 1952 by the Batista regime. It also commented on the current political situation in Cuba, decrying "the restriction of liberty in all its aspects, the surveillance and persecutions . . . the determination demonstrated by the government in going against anything that would significantly better the working class . . . [and] the taxes that increase daily." The report ended by noting that events "force us libertarians . . . to confront the regime with all our forces; we will cooperate with initiatives that tend to return to the country the liberty it is currently denied."

In 1956 Cuba became totally polarized between Batista and his political enemies, including the electoral political parties. This was largely a result of his suspension of the 1940 constitution. The anarchists maintained their anti-dictatorial positions and denounced the disastrous politics of Batista. In this crucial year, the ALC published a pamphlet written by Marcelo Salinas and Casto Moscú titled *Proyecciones Libertarias* ("Libertarian Projections"), which denounced "the evil politics of Batista" while at the same time predicting what would emanate from the Sierras Orientales and Fidel Castro.

Already in 1957 at the 24th National Council of the CTC, Casto Moscú denounced the official report of the secretary general of that organization, Eusebio Mujal, which advocated that—in violation of the accords of the CTC—the organization undertake electoral party politicking inside the unions. As a result of the change in direction of the CTC, and in compliance with the "accords of our organization," two prominent anarchists resigned their positions in the CTC: Modesto Barbeito (Organizational Secretary) and Abelardo Iglesias (Cultural Secretary).

Despite the difficulties of these dark times, *Solidaridad Gastronómica* continued publishing monthly. That this periodical appeared in times of censorship and suspension of constitutional rights is a testament to the determination of the Cuban anarchists. *Solidaridad Gastronómica* could be characterized as both viscerally anti-communist and anti-fascist, and it zealously defended "libertarian socialism." Its directors were Juan R. Álvarez, Domingo Alonso, and Manuel González, and its offices remained at the end of the decade at Jesús María 310, the offices of the ALC.

On April 14, 1957, the Conferencia Anarquista de las Américas was celebrated in Montevideo, Uruguay. The ALC sent Casto Moscú and José A. Álvarez as its representatives. Among other things, this conference denounced all of the dictatorships plaguing Latin America, including the one in Cuba.

At about the same time another revolutionary stage opened at the headquarters of the ALC, a place which was often the site of clandestine meetings. Among those conspiring were openly insurrectionary groups such as the Directorio Revolucionario (Revolutionary Directorate, a social-democratic group) and M26J. The ALC headquarters was raided on a number of occasions by Batista's police, though without much success for their repressive purposes.

Anarchists involved in insurrectional activities included Gilberto Lima and Luis Linsuaín, who were part of M26J. The underground movement was divided into zones, and Lima participated in the urban armed struggle in the Havana-Matanzas area, and Linsuaín took part in guerrilla activity in the northern part of Oriente Province. Another anarchist, Plácido Méndez, was active in the Segundo Frente (Second Front) guerrilla campaign in the Escambray Mountains. These were but a few of the many anarchists participating in armed actions at this time.

The anarchists were, of course, persecuted for their part in the armed struggle. Gilberto Lima was jailed and tortured on several occasions, and Isidro Moscú was viciously tortured, almost to death. According to Casto Moscú, Isidro was taken prisoner and tortured along with a number of other compañeros who had been preparing an armed uprising in Pinar del Rio Province. Juan R. Álvarez, Roberto Bretau, Luis Linsuaín, Plácido Méndez, Claudio Martínez, and Modesto Barbeito were also arrested, along with many other anarchists. Álvarez, Barbeito, and Aquiles Iglesias went into exile after they were released from prison.

By the middle of 1958, the Cuban capitalist elite began to comprehend that Batista and his repressive apparatus were at the point of losing power. This privileged group, along with U.S. interests, felt threatened and no longer considered Batista an ally. So, they decided to support the opposition to Batista. Castro obtained several million dollars from them to buy arms. This money came from big industrialists and big businesses, such as Hermanos Babun Ship Builders, and Bacardi Rum, as a reward for Castro's having resisted Batista in the mountains of Oriente Province for two years. (Batista had ordered a well-calculated "persecution" of Castro, designed not to extinguish the rebellion, but rather to evade its political ends.) At this time, the highest Cuban economic spheres considered Castro as the solution to the then-current crisis, and as a potential ally. He certainly appeared so. His armed uprising, known as "the struggle against the dictatorship" (despite later propaganda), never had a solid campesino base, let alone a proletarian base. It was, rather, in good part the work of capitalism and the Cuban bourgeoisie.

In 1957 and 1958 there were several armed actions: a naval uprising at Cienfuegos, an attack on the Goicuría Barracks in Matanzas, a landing on the north coast of Oriente Province, and an attempted assassination of Batista in the so-called "Palace Attack." All of these failed miserably, costing many lives. At the same time, an independent guerrilla uprising occurred in the mountains of Escambray in the central part of Cuba. A number of armed groups were active in the province of Las Villas, especially in the mountainous part of the province. These included the Directorio Revolucionario (Revolutionary Directorate) and the Segundo Frente del Escambray (Second Front of Escambray). Many of those participating were veterans of urban combat seeking refuge in the mountains; there were also many campesinos disaffected from the government, who didn't do much in the way of armed actions, but who kept the government's troops tied up for months. For its part, M26J had nothing to do with these events, and they were publicly and openly repudiated by Fidel Castro.

By the middle of 1958, Batista had lost the political battle and could no longer militarily contain the rebels. Washington turned its back on him and would no longer sell him arms.[3] At the same time, members of the Cuban Communist Party traveled to Castro's camp in the Sierra Maestra and began making deals with like-minded rebels, and later with Castro personally. The bearded leader grew politically stronger every day, and signed a pact in Caracas, Venezuela with all opposition elements, all of whom evidently admired him. Castro's economic, social, and political program continued being the same— at least he declared it so—as in 1953: social justice, electoral-political reform, and the re-implementation of the well-respected Constitution of 1940.

Finally, Batista fled Cuba on December 31, 1958. Another historical cycle had begun for Cuba's libertarians.

---

3. The policy of the U.S. government since the 1920s has been to sell any government (dictatorial or not) in Latin America arms, ammunition, ships, and planes (though not the latest models) if it helps to maintain the status quo. This continues to the present day, with, for example, the Army's School of the America's providing instruction on torture, counter-intelligence, and political assassination.

4

Castroism & Confrontation
(1959–1961)

Cuba's anarchists had actively participated in the struggle against the Batista dictatorship. Some had fought as guerrillas in the eastern mountains and in those of Escambray in the center of the island; others had taken part in the urban struggle. Their purposes were the same as those of the majority of the Cuban people: to oust the military dictatorship and to end political corruption. In addition to considering these ends desirable in and of themselves, the anarchists believed they would provide a wider space in which to work in the ideological, social, and labor fields. No one expected a radical change in the socioeconomic structure of the country.

The previously mentioned 1956 pamphlet, *Proyecciones Libertarias,* which attacked Batista, also characterized Castro as someone who merited "no confidence whatsoever," because "he [didn't] respect promises and only fought for power." It was for this reason that the anarchists established frequent clandestine contacts with other revolutionary groups, especially the Directorio Revolucionario, although there were also contacts with libertarian elements such as Gilberto Lima within M26J. Many of these meetings were held secretly at the ALC offices at Calle Jesús María 103 for the purposes of coordination of sabotage activities and of facilitating the distribution of opposition propaganda.

Upon the triumph of the revolution, Castro had become the indisputable leader of the revolutionary process, largely as a result of an incorrect evaluation by Batista's political opposition, which regarded Castro as a necessary, temporary, and controllable evil.

If the libertarians were uneasy about Castro, the rest of the political opposition, the Cuban capitalist elite, and the U.S. embassy expected to manipulate him. For their part, the majority of the Cuban people supported Castro without reserve in the midst of unprecedented jubilation. It appeared to them that they were at the portal of paradise, when in reality it was the antechamber of the inferno.

Due to the apparent refusal of Castro to lead, a "revolutionary government" was created with his support, the purpose of which was to "settle accounts" with the criminals of the former government. "Revolutionary Tribunals" were established which issued summary judgments in response to "popular demand." These tribunals handed down lengthy prison terms and death sentences, thus reestablishing the death penalty (which had been abolished by the Constitution of 1940), but this time for political crimes.

The leaders of the new revolutionary government understood the importance of the Cuban working class, which was simultaneously organized under and made superfluous by the political groups and reformists who controlled the CTC. They had learned this lesson through one notable failure. In April 1958, M26J had ordered a general strike in Havana, but it was badly organized, and the coordination with other revolutionary groups was also bad. As a result, the strike roundly failed, which served to demonstrate that M26J had essentially no base in the unions or among the working class. Given this experience, upon taking power one of the first goals of Castro's "revolutionary" government was taking control of the CTC (which they quickly renamed the Confederación de Trabajadores de Cuba Revolucionaria—CTCR).[1]

In the first days of January 1959—using the excuse of purging the CTC of collaborators with the old regime—the new government arbitrarily expelled all of the leading anarcho-syndicalists from the gastronomic, transport, construction, electrical utility, and other unions of the confederation. Some of these individuals had actively opposed the dictatorship, and others had suffered prison and exile. Three outstanding libertarian militants who fell victim to this purge were Santiago Cobo, from the transport workers' union, Casto Moscú, from the gastronomic workers' union, and Abelardo Iglesias, from the construction workers' union. In all three cases rank-and-file fellow workers came forward to defend them; if they hadn't done this, Cobo, Moscú, and Iglesias would have ended up in prison. This purge gravely affected the already weakened libertarians, even though the anarcho-syndicalist movement retained its prestige among the Cuban proletariat.

But the purge was not comprehensive. The new regime couldn't eliminate wholesale the many union leaders who had remained

---

1. This was typical of the omnipresent renaming process. To cite but two examples of this process, the Fuerzas Armadas (Armed Forces) became the Fuerzas Armadas Revolucionarias, and the navy, Marina de Guerra, became the Marina de Guerra Revolucionaria.

neutral in the conflict between Castro and Batista. There still remained within the CTCR leaders who had the backing of Cuba's workers, and others who had been forced to go into exile under Batista's dictatorship.

Despite the purge, the libertarian publications *Solidaridad Gastronómica* and *El Libertario* initially adopted a favorable, but cautious and expectant, attitude toward the new revolutionary government. However, the national council of the ALC issued a manifesto in which it "expounded on . . . and passed judgment on the triumphant Cuban revolution." After explaining the libertarian opposition to the past dictatorship, the manifesto analyzed the present and near future, declaring that the "revolutionary" institutional changes did not merit enthusiasm, and that one should have no illusions about them. It stated, with a certain irony, that its authors were "sure that for some time at least we'll enjoy public liberties sufficient to guarantee the opportunity of publishing propaganda." It went on with a well-aimed attack against "state centralism," saying that it would lead to an "authoritarian order," and it then made reference to the penetration of the Catholic Church and the Communist Party in the "revolutionary" process. It concluded with a reference to the workers' movement, where it noted the emphasis of the PCC on "reclaiming the hegemony which . . . it enjoyed during the other era of Batista's domination," even though it predicted that this would not occur. The manifesto ended on a note of optimism: "The panorama, despite all, is encouraging."

For its part, and taking a similar tack, *Solidaridad Gastronómica* on February 15, 1959 published another manifesto to Cuba's workers and the people in general in which it warned that a revolutionary government was an impossibility, and that "[in order] that rights and liberties are respected and exercised . . . it's necessary that union elections be called . . . and that [workers'] assemblies begin to function." It later noted that the decision of relieving past officers of their duties "must absolutely be that of the workers themselves . . . since to do this in any other way would be to fall into the procedures of the past . . . We'll combat this." Unfortunately, this manifesto didn't resonate in the Cuban working class.

In its March 15, 1959 issue, *Solidaridad Gastronómica* bitterly condemned "the dictatorial proceedings [of the CTCR] . . . agreements and mandates handed down from the top that impose measures, dismiss and install [union] directors." The paper also accused "elements . . . in the assemblies who are not members of the unions" of "raising their arms in favor of orders of the [new] directors."

Among other abnormalities it cited the following: "On occasions the assembly halls have been filled with armed militia men, which constitutes a blatant form of coercion and lack of respect for regulatory precepts," and which shows that the marxists "will resort to any type of proceeding to maintain their control of the unions." As is obvious in hindsight, the battle to liberate the unions was lost despite the denunciations of the anarcho-syndicalists.

The opposition to anarcho-syndicalism emanated directly from M26J and was instigated by the PCC elements which had infiltrated it and had in an almost military manner quickly taken control of all of the unions on the island. They said that they had done this as a temporary measure in order to purge the corrupt elements left in the unions from the Batista dictatorship, and that their domination would last only until there were new union elections. But as has so often been the case in Cuba, the "temporary" became permanent.

But where did the M26J elements who took over the unions come from? It was well known that M26J had never had a real base in the unions, had not had even the general sympathy of the workers, and didn't have working class leadership.

The "revolutionary" union directors came in a majority of cases from two antagonistic camps. One camp was the syndicalist Comisiones Obreras (the reformist Workers' Commissions), which tied itself to electoral politics and whose members had been enemies of the Batista regime; the Comisiones Obreras belonged to the Partido del Pueblo Ortodoxo and to the Partido Revolucionario Cubano Auténtico. The Comisiones had been founded in the late 1940s, and both parties had been well known from the founding of the CTC in 1939. They shared a visceral and profound anti-Communism. The other camp was the PCC. The former engaged in cynical opportunism and lent itself to any type of state manipulation. The latter was extremely dangerous, and despite its muddy past received even in the very early stages official support from the highest levels of government. Both sides hated the other, and they were preparing for an open struggle for hegemony in the proletarian sector; but instead, as we'll see later, this whole affair ended in an amalgamation disastrous to the Cuban workers' movement.

By July 1959, the Cuban state was totally in the hands of Castro and his close advisers, almost all of whom had come directly from the armed struggle against Batista. The presence of the PCC was already notable among the leading government figures, notably in Fidel's brother Raúl and in Ernesto Guevara, both of whom were openly marxist-leninist. Such a glaring fact provoked a reaction in Cuba's political climate, which had been characterized by anti-Communism. The anarchists had noted the influence of the PCC and were greatly alarmed, because they understood that the PCC's influence in the governmental and union spheres would lead to a mortal blow to both anarchism and workers' autonomy sooner or later. Their nightmares would shortly become reality. For his part, Castro publicly declared that he had no relationship with the PCC, but that he had Communists in his government, just as he had anti-Communists in it.

The situation of these last turned critical in the final days of 1959. Halfway through the year the political adversaries of Castro had already begun to take note of the growing PCC influence, and began a timid opposition campaign—which they understood as their right and duty—against what they called "the Communist infiltration of the government." The response was draconian. They were labeled seditious "enemies of the revolution" and "agents of Yankee imperialism." Treated as such, they were jailed or forced into exile.

The first victim of this Machiavellian maneuvering was Manuel Urrutía. Urrutía, a former judge in Santiago de Cuba, and an M26J sympathizer and anti-Communist, was named by M26J as *de facto* president of the revolutionary government following Batista's overthrow. Pressed by the ministers in his own government (including Fidel Castro) to name Castro as "máximo lider de la Revolución" ("maximum leader of the revolution"), Urrutía refused. He was then forced to resign and seek asylum in a foreign embassy following false accusations of corruption.

A worse fate awaited one of his closest political allies and a member of his cabinet. Humberto Sorí Marín, the former commander of the rebel army, the author of the agrarian reform law, and an anti-Communist, was jailed under the accusation of "conspiring against the revolution" and was executed in April 1961. Another ex-rebel commander also met an unkind fate. Hubert Matos, former military chief of the Camagüey district, complained to Castro himself about "Communist infiltration" in the ranks of the armed forces. He was then accused of sedition and later of treason for the crime of having resigned his rank and his post. He was sentenced to 20 years in prison, and served 16.

Then there was the case of Pedro Luis Díaz Lanz, head of the rebel air force. Preoccupied with the evident Communist influence within the Fuerzas Armadas Revolucionarias, Díaz Lanz discovered a marxist indoctrination center at a ranch near Havana called "El Cortijo" ("The Farmhouse"). He complained about this to Castro. In response, Castro forbade him from making this news public. Díaz Lanz became ever more disturbed by the increasing power of the PCC in both the armed forces and government, and resigned his post. He managed to escape to Miami before meeting a fate similar to those of Sorí Marín and Matos.

The reaction of parts of the opposition to this governmental repression was violent—sabotage and a few bombings. These clandestine actions were carried out by various political organizations, which at first were anti-Communist and in the end were anti-Castro. Almost all of these groups had been involved in the armed struggle against Batista and had been affiliated with M26J; they chose direct action because of the undeniable and growing marxist influence at the highest levels of the government. They sabotaged electric utilities, burned several shops and department stores, set off bombs in public places, and collected arms and explosives to send to guerrillas operating in the Escambray Mountains and also in the Sierra de los Órganos (despite there being as yet no united guerrilla front).

Castro's response to all this was predictable: he reestablished the "Revolutionary Tribunals" which handed down sentences of death by firing squad to anyone accused of "subversive acts." Thus commenced a long period of terror and counter-terror.

Meanwhile the international anarchist community was mourning the loss of Camilo Cienfuegos, the valiant veteran of the armed struggle, whose disappearance remained shrouded in mystery. Camilo was one of the children of Ramón Cienfuegos, a Cuban worker who had participated in the anarchist movement during the 1920s. He worked with the SIA and participated in the founding of the ALC, but according to Casto Moscú, "We never saw him again until Camilo became a national hero." The disappearance of Camilo was lamented by nearly the entire Cuban people, and also abroad by many libertarians who considered him an anarchist (though the truth is that he was never a member of the Cuban anarchist movement). Nonetheless, half the anarchist world cried over the loss of this revolutionary hero as if he had been another Durruti.[2] This is hardly surprising given that the Cuban government occupied itself (principally in Europe) with repeating to the point of fatigue that Comandante Camilo Cienfuegos was a libertarian militant, for the purpose of gaining support for the Castro regime within the international anarchist movement. The myth has persisted among libertarians to this day: Saint Camilo, the Anarchist.

---

2. Buenaventura Durruti (1896–1936) was a leading member of the militant Federación Anarquista de Ibérica. He was killed on the Madrid front while fighting fascists during the Spanish Civil War.

At the end of 1959, the Tenth National Congress of the Con-federación de Trabajadores de Cuba Revolucionaria (CTCR, the renamed CTC) was convened. A majority of the delegates accepted the goal of "Humanism," a type of philosophy which had been outlined at the beginning of the year as a means of distancing the CTCR from the traditional capitalist and Communist Cold War camps. The slogans of this Cuban Humanism were "Bread with Liberty" and "Liberty without Terror." The Cubans, with typical creativity, had invented a new socio-political system in order to give some type of ideological explanation for the new regime.[3] David Salvador, leader of the M26J faction, feigned and functioned as the most daring champion of this new Cuban "Humanism." For its part, the PCC, which was well represented in this Congress, though in the minority, called up the musty slogan, "Unity."

On November 23, the Congress found itself totally divided over the matters of making agreements and of electing representatives.[4] Confusion reigned, owing to the inability of the various opposing sectors to reach agreements. There were 2854 delegates at the Congress, of which the Communists only influenced 265. With that few delegates, it was impossible for them to control the Congress. But they had the backing of the revolutionary government and its new Minister of Labor, Augusto Martínez Sánchez, commander of the army and an intimate of Raúl Castro, the number two man in the new Cuban hierarchy (and just incidentally the number one man's brother).

The marxists then proposed the creation of a single list of candidates that would assume direction of the CTCR. That is to say,

---

3. "Humanism" meant, or at least implied, respect for human rights; political, social, and religious liberty; racial and social justice; and the rescuing of the Cuban campesino from misery through agrarian reform—in the end, it promised the creation of an idyllic Cuban state far different from any others existing in the hemisphere. The various anti-Communist union leaders had advanced this concept as a means of combatting marxist influence within the CTC. For their part, the Cuban anarchists—along with the people in general and the working class in particular—didn't pay much attention to "Humanism."

4. The ALC had already published a "Call to the 10th Congress" on the 15th of November in *Solidaridad Gastronómica*, in which it insisted that "The [CTC] congresses we've suffered for so long have had as the only question of importance the distribution of posts in the [CTC] apparatus." The ALC "Call" ended on an upbeat note: "[We would hope that this Congress] will mark a step forward in revolutionary syndicalism"; and it went on to express the hope that the Congress would "delve deeply into the grand proletarian questions, rather than personalities or sectarian matters." Of course, nothing came of this.

they proposed that control of the CTCR be put in the hands of a committee in which they (the PCC) would have equal representation with M26J and the anti-Communist unionists. Given their small representation within the union movement, this maneuver couldn't have been more cynical. Much to the surprise of Martínez Sánchez and Raúl Castro, both the independent unionists and the M26J faction rejected this proposal, with the M26J delegates whistling and shouting down their own leaders.

In light of the obvious paralysis created by the divisions in the Congress, Castro himself showed up and explained the importance of "defending the revolution," for which it was necessary that there be "truly revolutionary directors" supported by all the delegates of the Congress. He proposed that the CTCR leader be David Salvador, leader of the M26J contingent. The only faction that should prevail is "the party of the fatherland," said Castro. And effectively, as in the "good times" of the Cuban republic, as much as many wanted to forget them, the government of the day nominated the Secretary General of the CTCR. Salvador was then elected and given the task of designating a new "national directorate." Castro's nomination of Salvador in effect made him a governmental appendage, if not a government minister. On November 25, the Congress ended. The CTCR was now in the hands of the "independent" unionists who followed the government line.

It was logical that the syndicalist representatives of the M26J who opposed PCC control of the Congress and the CTCR, after listening to the instructions from their maximum leader, Fidel, about control of the organization, would mutely accept the government imposition of Salvador. This was for the simple reason that the orders coming from above indicated that they either comply or end up in jail. As the slogan of the day put it, "Fatherland or Death! We Will Win!" In this manner, a century of struggle by Cuban workers against the abuses of the bosses ended with the "Congress of the melons" (olive-green on the outside, the color of M26J's army uniforms, and red on the inside, the color of the PCC). The struggle against the individual bosses had ended, and in a few months the Cuban state would be the one and only boss—and a boss which controlled (and castrated) the only organization capable of defending workers' rights against it.

The 10th Congress marked the end of a nearly century-long history of workers' struggles, of strikes, of work stoppages that had begun with the first workers' associations in 1865. Twenty years later these associations became militant unions in the incipient Cuban anarcho-syndicalist movement, with their tobacco strikes, demonstrations, congresses, free schools, newspapers, and other activities. Until a few months after the founding of the CNOC (at the time, frankly anarcho-syndicalist) in 1925, the Cuban workers' movement aimed toward apoliticism and against the participation of the movement's leaders in elections or political office.

The arrival of the PCC and its opportunistic assault aimed at taking over the CNOC, in order to put it at the disposition of Machado in 1933 and Batista in 1939, is a bench mark in the lethal fossilization of the Cuban workers' movement.

The control of the CTC by elements affiliated with Eusebio Mujal during the entire decade of the 1950s was another backward step for workers' emancipation. But the 10th Congress of the CTCR was the crushing blow. After it, the Cuban proletariat would be firmly harnessed to the government cart.

At the end of that 10th Congress, *Solidaridad Gastronómica* commented in a December 15, 1960 editorial titled "Considerations Concerning the 10th Congress of the CTCR" that, "It was demonstrated at the Congress that the marxist señores not only do not represent a force inside the Cuban workers' movement, but that the repulsion they inspire in the proletariat of our country is well known." Later, the editorial continued: "This underlines once more the inclination toward total control of the workers' movement by the political current that rules the nation." It ended on a totally unfounded optimistic note: "The 10th Cuban Workers' Congress didn't deliver leadership of the organization to the Communists, an indisputable proof that the proletariat can't be easily fooled."[5]

The new directorate named by Salvador dedicated itself to "purifying" the unions and federation of all of the anti-Communist elements who had resisted the marxists at the Congress. Already by April 1960 this "purification" had achieved results as satisfactory to the government as to the PCC.

One result was the militarization of the labor force. The CTCR pressured the unions and federations to create militias. Because union membership was obligatory in all workplaces, this in effect forced Cuba's workers to "voluntarily" militarize themselves.

While this was occurring, David Salvador, pressured by both the

---

5. Earlier in the year, the anarcho-syndicalists had noted more astutely in an editorial on February 15th in the same paper that then new "Organic Law of the Ministry of Work" would, in the name of "greater security" and "justice," "lead to the nullification of syndicalist action and would also deliver the power of decision on all workers' matters to the state apparatus. . . . [It would] establish the paternalism of the state and the servility of the workers."

"directorate" he had named and by the Secretary of Labor, Martínez Sánchez, resigned his post. (Ironically, the English translation of "Salvador" is "Savior.") A few weeks later it was filled by PCC member Lázaro Peña. A little after this, Salvador, the man who had delivered the Cuban working class to Fidel Castro, was detained on suspicion of "counter-revolutionary activities." Shortly after he was released, he went into exile, where he continues to live in obscurity.

These were difficult times, as in any revolutionary process in which the people debate among themselves amidst fear, hope, and uncertainty. Matters were worse for the anarchists than for most other Cubans, as at the start of the year the official Castro organ, *Revolución*, had begun a campaign of anti-anarchist provocation, making accusations that were as veiled as they were false. The PCC had not only seized control of the unions, but the government was vilifying the strongest defenders of workers' rights.

On January 25, 1960, the ALC held a national assembly. Its accords included a call to "support the Cuban Revolution" because of "its indisputable benefit to the people," its delivery of "more social justice and enjoyment of liberty." Nonetheless, in the same paragraph it expressed the ALC's "total rejection of all types of imperialism, totalitarianism, and dictatorships, the world over." The accords also included a call for support of and solidarity with "el compañero Casto Moscú . . . [in the face of] sectarian attacks and calumnies." The ALC delegates also elected a new national council, with José Rodriguez González as Secretary General. Others named to positions of responsibility included Rolando Piñera Pardo, Bernardo Moreno, Manuel Gaona, Marcelo Álvarez, and Omar Dieguez.

Later that year, just before falling victim to "revolutionary" censorship, *Solidaridad Gastronómica*, the ALC journal, published its final issue. That issue, of December 15, 1960, contained a front page article commemorating Durruti's death during the defense of Madrid. In it, *Solidaridad* noted, "A dictatorship can originate in the politics of class domination." An editorial in the same issue stated:

> A collective dictatorship . . . of the working class, or to use the terminology of the day, a people's dictatorship, would be a contradiction in terms, given that the characteristic of all dictatorships, including "peoples'" or "proletarian," is the placing of power in the hands of a few persons—not its sharing by the populace. Dictators have absolute dominion not only over the oppressed political and social classes, but above all over the members of the supposed dominant class. The day will never come when there is a dictatorship of workers or proletarians, campesinos and students . . . or whatever

you want to call it . . . The power of dictators falls upon all . . . not only upon industrialists, landowners, and plantation owners . . . but also upon the proletariat and the people in general—and also upon those "revolutionaries" who do not directly participate in the exercise of power.

As for non-Cuban anarchist analyses of the situation, the German libertarian Agustín Souchy journeyed to Havana in the summer of 1960. Souchy had been invited by the government to study the situation of Cuban agriculture and to issue his opinions on it, and many anarchists were enthusiastic about his visit. The German writer was warmly greeted by Cuba's anarchists on August 15, 1960.

Souchy was a student of agriculture and had written a widely known (in Europe) pamphlet, *The Israeli Cooperatives*, about the organization of the kibbutzim. This was the reason that the Cuban government had invited him to visit Cuba—it expected something similar from him; it hoped that he would write an endorsement of its gigantic agrarian program which would, among other things, be useful as propaganda in the anarchist media and among libertarian Cubans.

This didn't happen. Souchy traveled the island with his eyes wide open, and his analysis of the situation couldn't have been more pessimistic. He concluded that Cuba was going too near the Soviet model, and that the lack of individual freedom and individual initiative could lead to nothing but centralism in the agricultural sector, as was already notable in the rest of the economy. His analysis was issued in a pamphlet titled *Testimonios sobre la Revolución Cubana*, which was published without going through official censorship. Three days after Souchy left the island, the entire print run of the pamphlet was seized and destroyed by the Castro government, on the suggestion of the PCC leadership. Fortunately, this attempt at suppression was only partially successful, as the anarchist publisher Editorial Reconstruir in Buenos Aires issued a new printing of the work in December 1960, with a new prologue by Jacobo Prince.

In this same summer of 1960, convinced that Castro inclined more each day toward a marxist-leninist government which would asphyxiate freedom of expression, communication, association, and even movement, the majority in the ALC agreed to issue its *Declaración de Principios* under another name. This document was signed by the Grupo de Sindicalistas Libertarios and was endorsed by the Agrupación Sindicalista Libertaria in June. The reason for using this name was to avoid reprisals against members of the ALC. This document is vital in understanding the situation of the Cuban anarchists at this time. Its objectives included informing the Cuban people of the political and social situation, accusing the government of fomenting disaster, and engaging the PCC—many of whose members were already occupying important positions in the government—in debate.

The eight points of the *Declaración* attacked "the state in all its forms": 1) it defined, in accord with libertarian ideas, the functions of unions and federations in regard to their true economic roles; 2) it declared that the land should belong "to those who work it"; 3) it backed "cooperative and collective work" in contrast to the agricultural centralism of the government's Agrarian Reform law; 4) it called for the free and collective education of children; 5) it inveighed against "noxious" nationalism, militarism, and imperialism, opposing fully the militarization of the people; 6) it attacked "bureaucratic centralism" and weighed forth in favor of federalism; 7) it proposed individual liberty as a means of obtaining collective liberty; and 8) it declared that the Cuban Revolution was, like the sea, "for everyone," and energetically denounced "the authoritarian tendencies that surge in the breast of the revolution."

This was one of the first direct attacks against the regime's ideological viewpoint. The response wasn't long in coming. In August 1960, the organ of the PCC, *Hoy* ("Today"), under the signature of Secretary General Blas Roca, the most prominent leader in the Communist camp, responded to the *Declaración* in *ad hominem* manner, repeating the same libels as the PCC had used in 1934, and adding the dangerous accusation that the authors of the *Declaración* were "agents of the Yankee State Department." According to one of the authors of the *Declaración*, Abelardo Iglesias, "in the end, the ex-friend of Batista, Blas Roca, answered us in [*Hoy's*] Sunday supplement, showering us with insults."

It's most significant that an attack on the Castro government was answered by one of the highest leaders in the PCC rather than by a government official. In the summer of 1960, any doubts that existed about the government's direction began to fade. From this moment, anarchists who were enemies of the regime had to engage in clandestine operations. They attempted to have a 50-page pamphlet printed in reply to the PCC and Blas Roca, but, according to Iglesias, "we couldn't get our printers—already terrorized by the dictatorship —to print it. Neither could we manage a clandestine edition."[6]

---

6. A month before this *El Libertario* had dedicated its July 19th edition to a "celebration of the heroic attitude of the anarchists in July 1936" at the start of the Spanish Civil War/Revolution. The members of the Spanish Confederación Nacional del Trabajo in exile in Havana, enthusiastic about the triumph of the Cuban

The most combative elements among the Cuban anarchists had few options left at their disposal. After the response to the *Declaración,* they knew that they would be harried by the government, as would be any other Cubans opposed to the "revolutionary" process. In those days an accusation of being "counter-revolutionary" meant a trip to jail or to the firing squad. So, with other means cut off, they went underground and resorted to clandestine direct action.

Their reasons are as valid today as they were then. As we have seen, anarcho-syndicalism within the Cuban unions and federations had been suppressed. Freedom of the press had been suspended, and it was dangerous to have opinions contrary to those of the government. To attack the government verbally was an attack against the homeland. And the regime's politico-economic policies were quickly leading to the Sovietization of Cuba, with all its negative consequences.

The regime was conducting this economic campaign with rigor, and had gone after all of the big businesses, ranches, sugar mills, tobacco fields, etc. In other words, it was confiscating all of the national wealth that until this time had been in the hands of the big bourgeoisie, national capitalism, and U.S./Cuban banking. The anarchists didn't criticize these "nationalization" measures. What they opposed was *state* ownership/dictatorship over all of Cuba's wealth.

What was left for Cuba's anarchists was to choose either the hard path of exile or that of clandestine struggle. As Casto Moscú would explain, "We were convinced that all of our efforts and those of our people had gone for nothing, and that we had arrived at a worse, more menacing situation than all of the ills we had already combatted." Facing this totalitarian situation, the great majority of Cuba's anarchists decided to rebel. They initiated an armed struggle that was condemned from the start to failure.

Among nonviolent anarchist opposition activities at this time was the clandestine bulletin, *MAS* (*Movimiento de Acción Sindical*),[7] which circulated throughout the island and overseas. *MAS* featured in its few monthly editions (August–December 1960) attack without quarter

---

Revolution, had proposed the violent overthrow of Spanish dictator Francisco Franco. In this same edition, dedicated to defending the libertarian attitude before, during, and after the Spanish Civil War, a sincere but almost pathetic afterthought appeared on the final page: an account of the activities of the ALC in the struggle against Batista. The inventory was long, and it pointedly reminded the government of the support of the anarchists' for the revolution and for liberty. This was the last cartridge in the anarchists ideological arsenal, and it did no good. *El Libertario* disappeared for good that same summer.

7. The acronym "MAS" means "more" in Spanish.

against the PCC and its followers in general and against Castro in particular. As for the situation in Cuba at this time, Casto Moscú states: "An infinity of manifestos were written denouncing the false postulates of the Castro revolution and calling the populace to oppose it. Many meetings were held to debate matters and to raise awareness," and "plans were put into effect to sabotage the basic things sustaining the state."

The methods included armed struggle. Moscú relates: "I participated in efforts to support guerrilla insurgencies in different parts of the country." In particular, two important operations took place in the same zone, the Sierra Occidental, in which operations were difficult because the mountains aren't very high, they're narrow, and they're near Havana: "There was direct contact with the guerrilla band commanded by Captain Pedro Sánchez in San Cristobal; since some of our compañeros participated actively in this band . . . they were supplied with arms . . . We also did everything we could to support the guerrilla band commanded by Francisco Robaina (known as 'Machete') that operated in the same range." At least one anarchist fighter in these bands, Augusto Sánchez, was executed by the government without trial after being taken prisoner. The government considered the guerrillas "bandits" and had very little respect for the lives of those who surrendered.

According to Moscú, in addition to Augusto Sánchez, the following "compañeros combatientes" were murdered by the Castro government: Rolando Tamargo, Sebastián Aguilar, Jr. and Ventura Suárez were shot; Eusebio Otero was found dead in his cell; Raúl Negrin, harassed beyond endurance, set himself on fire. Many others were arrested and sent to prison, among them Modesto Piñeiro, Floreal Barrera, Suria Linsuaín, Manuel González, José Aceña, Isidro Moscú, Norberto Torres, Sicinio Torres, José Mandado Marcos, Plácido Méndez, and Luis Linsuaín, these last two being officials in the Rebel Army. Francisco Aguirre died in prison; Victoriano Hernández, sick and blind because of prison tortures, killed himself; and José Álvarez Micheltorena died a few weeks after getting out of prison.

The situation of Cuba's libertarians grew more tense with each passing day. The failed Bay of Pigs invasion, in Playa Giron, south of Matanzas Province, on the 17th of April 1961—an adventure as well financed as it was badly planned by the CIA—gave the government the excuse it needed to totally liquidate the internal opposition, which of course included the anarchists, and to consolidate its power.

On May Day, 1961, Castro declared his government "socialist" —in practice, stalinist. This presented the libertarians both inside and outside of Cuba with an ethical dilemma: the regime demanded the most decided allegiance of its sympathizers and militants, and didn't recognize abstention or a neutral position. This meant that one either slept with criminals or died of insomnia, that is, one either supported the regime, went into exile, or went into the cemetery.

In previous epochs, there were other routes. In the 19th century, one could either opt for the separatist forces or keep out of the independence question. When Machado or Batista were in power, the libertarians could declare themselves anti-political or pass over to the opposition groups with the most affinity for anarchist ideals—left revolutionaries or liberal or social-democratic political groups. But the Third Republic, presided over by a budding dictator, offered only four alternatives: placing oneself under the dictator's control; prison; the firing squad; or exile.

A few months after Fidel Castro declared himself a marxist-leninist, an event without parallel in the history of Cuban anarchism occurred. Manuel Gaona Sousa, an old railroad worker from the times of Enrique Varona and the CNOC, a libertarian militant his entire life and a founder of the ALC, and in the first years of Castroism the ALC's Secretary of Relations—and hence the person dealing with overseas anarchist media and organizations—betrayed both his ideals and his comrades. In a document titled *A Clarification and a Declaration of the Cuban Libertarians*, dated and signed in Marianao on November 24, 1961, Gaona denounced the Cuban anarchists who didn't share his enthusiasm for the Castro revolution.[8]

After the first confrontations with the most stalinist sectors of the PCC, it was understood in the ALC that the regime, on its way to totalitarianism, would not permit the existence of an anarchist organization, or even the propagation of anarchist ideas. The PCC wanted to settle accounts with the anarchists. For his part, Gaona preferred to save his own skin by settling in the enemy camp, leaving his former comrades to fend for themselves.

In all lands and all latitudes there have always been those who have embraced and then rejected libertarian ideas. In this, Gaona was not unusual. The renunciation of anarchism by prominent anarchists was nothing new; persons with equal or more responsibility than Gaona in Cuban anarchist organizations had done it, exchanging their social opinions for Cuban electoral politics. For example, Enrique Messonier crossed over to the Partido Liberal in 1901; Antonio

---

8. Following Castro's rise to power, Gaona had contributed consistently pro-Castro articles to the ALC journal, *Solidaridad Gastronómica*. It apparently mattered not a whit to him that Castro's government had suppressed that journal.

Penichet to the Partido Auténtico at the beginning of the 1930s; and Helio Nardo to the Partido Ortodoxo at the end of the 1940s. These acts were never considered traitorous by the majority of libertarian militants. They simply believed that these ex-compañeros had the right to choose their own political destiny, and those who switched allegiances were never anathematized. Besides, they hadn't drastically changed their basic positions, and they hadn't associated themselves with parties of the extreme right or with other totalitarian or religious parties. This wasn't the case with Gaona. He not only allied himself with the reactionary forces governing Cuba, but he also threatened to denounce as "agents of imperialism" former comrades who didn't share his pseudo-revolutionary posture to the recently formed Committees for the Defense of the Revolution—which, of course, would have meant prison or the firing squad for anyone he denounced.

Gaona went further and coerced several elderly anarchists, such as Rafael Serra and Francisco Bretau, into being accomplices in his betrayal through a document in which he attempted to "clarify" for overseas anarchists "an insidious campaign being waged in the libertarian press of your country . . . against the Cuban Revolution" with the purpose of "collecting money for the Cuban libertarian prisoners . . . to deliver them and their families out of the country." The document railed against what Gaona labeled "a hoax, irresponsibility, and bad faith" on the part of his ex-comrades now in exile or taking refuge in some embassy. He then guaranteed in the first paragraph that there did not exist on the entire island "a single libertarian comrade who has been detained or persecuted for his ideas." And this when Gaona had expelled all the anarchists from the ALC and dissolved the organization![9]

The second paragraph of Gaona's document declared that there didn't exist any type of political or religious persecution in Cuba, and then attempted to identify the Bay of Pigs prisoners with all of the opposition forces in Cuba, including, of course, the anarchists. To combat this threat, there existed an "extreme vigilance in the people through the Committees for the Defense of the Revolution—one on every block—against the terrorists." Gaona thus justified the terrorism of the state against the people through committees of informers that answered to the feared state security agency. He also implied that any citizen that didn't back this "revolutionary" process, these intrusive committees, was a traitor who deserved to be denounced.

---

9. The government did not set up a fake ALC with Gaona as its head, because, in all probability, it considered him a loose cannon who might become a problem in its future dealings with non-Cuban anarchists.

Gaona then lied outright when he declared that "almost the totality of libertarian militants in Cuba find themselves integrated into the distinct 'Organisms of the Cuban Revolution'," all of which he labeled "mass organizations." He then boasted that the "integration" of these militants was the "consequence of the molding [into reality] . . . of all of the immediate objectives of our program . . . and the reason for being of the international anarchist movement and the international workers' movement." Here one can grasp fully the intention and direction of this document. According to Gaona, the anarchists "integrated" themselves spontaneously into Castro's despotism because it embodied the objective of all of their social struggles over more than a century. He even goes beyond this and says that Castro's despotism embodies the true agenda and purpose of all of the world's anarchists.

Gaona ends with an exhortation to non-Cuban anarchists "to not be surprised by the bad intentions and false information that you'll receive from those . . . at the service, conscious or unconscious, of the Cuban counter-revolution, who undertake to remain deaf and blind before the realities . . . of the most progressive, democratic, and humanist Revolution of our continent." Finally, he states that it's necessary to support Castroism and "to take up arms" in its defense, declaring "traitors and cowards" those who "under the pretext of differences or sectarian rancor" oppose this beautiful dream.

This document is treated here at length because it will help the reader better understand its sinister consequences in coming years. Gaona, at the end of his life, had betrayed his comrades, but even worse, he coerced five elderly members of the Cuban anarchist movement—some already infirm octogenerians—into endorsing this monstrous declaration that precisely negated all libertarian principles, both inside and outside Cuba. Vicente Alea, Rafael Serra, Francisco Bretau, Andrés Pardo, and Francisco Calle ("Mata") signed this document along with 16 others who had little or nothing to do with Cuban anarchism.

Many libertarians still on the island rejected this bit of infamy and were thus considered enemies of the revolution; they were sooner or later forced to abandon their homeland. Among these was one of the most outstanding Cuban intellectuals, Marcelo Salinas, who, had he put himself at the service of the dictatorship by signing the Gaona document, would have received all of the honors and prestige that tyrants can deliver to their lackeys.

While Gaona was betraying his former comrades, two Cuban anarchists, Manuel González and Casto Moscú, who were involved in the transportation of arms and propaganda, were detained in Havana. Taken to a jail of the state security service and fearing that they would be shot—a common fate for "counter-revolutionaries"—they were put at liberty on the orders of the department commander, who was familiar with the work of the libertarians in the labor movement, and who mentioned with pride knowing Serra and Salinas in times past. González and Moscú wasted little time going directly from the jail to the Mexican embassy, where they were received almost without formalities. Both would march into exile via Mexico and would later reunite with their comrades in Miami.

5

Exile & Shadows

(1962–2001)

Even though some anarchists—whether or not involved in the violent opposition—had gone into exile as early as mid 1960, it wasn't until the summer of 1961 that a collective exodus began to the U.S. This wasn't the first time that Cuba's anarchists had found refuge in that country. Since the late 19th century, Key West, Tampa, and New York had been the places chosen by persecuted Cuban libertarians, because they offered the best opportunities of earning a living, and because the Florida cities were near enough to Cuba to continue the political struggle. During the Machado and Batista dictatorships, exiled anarchists had gone to these cities; and the Cuban anarchists had contacts with anarchist groups in other U.S. cities.

The U.S. immigration laws had stiffened against anarchists in the 1920s, and these laws were still in force in the early 1960s—as many would-be political refugees unjustly denied entrance will remember. But the Immigration and Naturalization Service made an exception for the Cuban anarchists fleeing the Castro dictatorship, evidently believing that "the enemy of my enemy is my friend," and that the Cuban anarchists were therefore potential allies. What is certain is that the U.S. authorities asked almost all of the new refugees about their political affiliations, that the Cuban libertarians were truthful about the matter, and that they were permitted entrance to and residency in the United States. It's also true that, as in other times, it was unusual to encounter a Cuban exile who thought of remaining in the U.S. for very long. All of the recently arrived, including the libertarians, were convinced that the return to Cuba was near and they planned their anti-Castro strategy accordingly.

In the summer of 1961, the Movimiento Libertario Cubano en el Exilio (MCLE) was formally constituted in New York by the not very numerous exiles in that city. At the same time, another libertarian group was organizing itself in Miami; this group included Claudio Martínez, Abelardo Iglesias, and Rolando Piñera, and was known as the Delegación General (of the MLCE). The New York section (of the MLCE) was composed almost entirely of members of the Sindicato Gastronómico, including Juan R. Álvarez, Floreal and Omar Diéguez, Bartolo García, Fernando Gómez, Manuel Rodríguez, and Juan Fidalgo. Fidalgo established, through Gómez, the first contacts with the exiled Spanish anarchists of the Club Aurora in Boston. At the time, another group of Spanish libertarian exiles in New York existed, centering around the long-running anarchist magazine, *Cultura Proletaria*; the Cubans also established good relations with this group.

But without doubt, the primary source of solidarity and coopera-tion for the newly arrived Cubans was the New York-based anarchist Libertarian League, led by Sam Dolgoff and Russell Blackwell. Blackwell had been a combatant in the Spanish Civil War and held notable responsibility in the American anarchist movement despite, or perhaps because of, his Trotskyist past.[1][2] Sam Dolgoff in those years was one of the most respected figures in North American anarchism, and after a long revolutionary career also had consider-able influence in the American left. Always at his side—and at times in front—was his compañera, Esther Dolgoff, who had also been involved in class-based anarchist politics since her youth. Another notable member of this group was Abe Bluestein, who also main-tained close relations with the Cubans. In 1954, this group had founded the Libertarian League, which had as its organ the newsletter titled *Views & Comments*. (Dick Ellington, mentioned in the footnote below, was a member of the group that produced this newsletter.) Without the collaboration of the members of the Libertarian League, the task of the Cuban anarchist exiles would have been much harder.

Already in this period collections were being taken among anarchists in the U.S., Mexico, Chile, Argentina, and almost all of Europe for the purpose of helping endangered Cuban anarchists and/or their families obtain visas and passage out of the country. The conditions of life in these years for the enemies of the regime were indescribable; they were suffering in the worst political prisons ever

---

1. Shortly before his death, Dick Ellington, the anarchist typesetter and friend of Russ Blackwell, told me that while fleeing Spain on his way back to New York, Blackwell had killed and thrown overboard two NKVD (Russian secret police) men sent to murder him on the ship carrying him home, and that following his return he was forced to live a semi-clandestine existence for several years for fear of his life. —CB

2. Because of both personal experience and political analysis, Blackwell renounced Trotskyism and became an anarchist—and perhaps one with better insight than most into the nature of marxism, because of his past marxist involvements. —FF

known in Cuba. They had to adapt themselves to inhuman conditions and suffered torment on a daily basis at the hands of their jailers— Cubans like themselves, who were engaging in cruelty in the name of "socialism." The desire to escape from this great dungeon that Cuba had become was an obsession for almost all Cubans.

The donations in August 1961 totaled $2088 (equivalent to about $11,600 today), and provoked the Gaona explosion (the DDG [Documento de Gaona], which denounced the exiled anarchists) in November. These funds, according to the bookkeeping records of Claudio Martínez, treasurer of the MLCE, came from many different places. For example, the comrades at *Freie Arbeiter Stimme*, the Yiddish anarchist paper in New York, contributed $425. Six hundred one dollars came from the SIA in Argentina. And many individuals also contributed, including Agustín Souchy and one Dutch anarchist, who stated that his donation was made for humanitarian reasons and that his sympathies remained with the Cuban Revolution. (This was typical of European anarchist confusion in regard to the Cuban anarchists and the Castro government.)

This collection brought more than 66 compañeros and family members to the U.S. at the same time as the Cuban anarchists in exile began a campaign to unmask the marxist-leninist regime afflicting Cuba. But to the astonishment of the Cuban anarchists, after initial success the financial appeal, which should have been further supported by those familiar with the Cuban problem, encountered difficulties. There were two principle reasons for the diminishing contributions: 1) the unexpected damage that the DDG document was doing in countries such as México, Venezuela, and Argentina; and 2) not all of the recently arrived Cubans in the U.S. responded to the appeals. In the face of this, by mid 1962 the MLCE had established a system of dues of $2 per month per member, which covered the most pressing costs, among them aid to recently arrived comrades and the campaign for Cuban political prisoners. And there were a number of these.

Cuba's anarchists suffered the same punishment as other Cubans accused of "counter-revolutionary" crimes. The abuse, maltreatment, and even torture of Cuba's political prisoners over the last four decades is well documented by Amnesty International and other human rights groups. In quality, this abuse was worse than that meted out to political prisoners in most other countries, as is indicated by the testimony of Marcelo Salinas (imprisoned in 1917–1918 in the U.S., Spain, and Cuba), Abelardo Iglesias (imprisoned in France in 1939), and Casto Moscú (imprisoned in Cuba in 1933). In such cases, if the accused accepted his sentence without too much protest and didn't make trouble in prison, the authorities generally freed the prisoner in the end, without abusing him too much physically.[3]

But that wasn't the case in Castro's Cuba. One major difference between the Castro regime and its predecessors was the sheer number of political prisoners. The Cuban writer Juan Clark notes: "According to a number of estimates, the highest number of political prisoners was 60,000 during the 1960s. Amnesty International estimates that by the mid 1970s the total number released was approximately 20,000." Of course, at the beginning of the Castro regime, there weren't enough prisons to house these huge numbers of political prisoners, so Castro embarked on a prison-construction campaign.

Curiously, according to political prisoners freed in the decade 1970–1980, the population of political prisoners in the "socialist" Cuban gulags came overwhelmingly from working class and campesino backgrounds. There should be no dispute about this, given the mass of evidence: the Castro regime persecuted its proletarian and campesino enemies far more vigorously than its capitalist enemies. Many anarchists suffered greatly under this policy.

The testimony of the anarchist former political prisoners Luis Linsuaín (originally condemned to death for attempting to assassinate Raúl Castro), Placido Méndez, and Isidro Moscú, all of whom served between 15 and 20 years imprisonment, outlines the abuses suffered by Castro's political foes. In the first years after the revolution, when the number of political prisoners far outstripped available prison space, prisoners lived in very cramped conditions. The treatment in Castro's prisons was (and apparently still is) brutal. Those slow to respond to orders were impelled to do so by being beaten with clubs or jabbed with bayonets. Prisoners were also forced to work in quarries or sugar cane fields, or to do other hard physical labor. The authorities also instituted a system imported from the USSR, under which prisoners who studied and attended classes on marxism-leninism received better treatment than those who resisted this carrot-and-stick system.

Those who refused to participate in this were labeled as dangerous "intransigents" by the authorities. These prisoners were so harassed that many resorted to hunger strikes and ended up in prison hos-

---

3. The abuse suffered by political prisoners in Castro's jails has been surpassed—perhaps—only by the abuse meted out to political prisoners in Brazil following the 1964 coup d'etat, in Chile following the 1973 coup, and in Argentina during the "dirty war" of the late 1970s and early 1980s. Not incidentally, there was heavy CIA involvement in all of these matters. —CB

pitals. Many of these, as well as other political prisoners—basically anyone accused of "antisocial conduct"—ended up buried in what in the U.S. would be called "the hole": extremely small cells, little bigger than a coffin, in which prisoners were held for days or even weeks.

On an individual note, we should mention the cases of Suria Linsuaín (sister of Luis, mentioned above) and Carmelina Casanova. The first of these was condemned for "counter-revolutionary" crimes to 30 years in the Guanajay and América Libre prisons. She completed five years imprisonment between 1964 and 1969, and was released from the prison hospital only when she was on the brink of death. Carmelina Casanova was also sentenced to 30 years imprisonment. Her crime was hiding anti-Castro militants. She completed eight years of her sentence before being released, and then fled to Miami, her health broken. She died shortly after her arrival. These are but two examples; at the minimum, hundreds of other anarchists suffered political imprisonment and mistreatment.

While aiding other libertarian political prisoners, the MLCE agitated to mobilize international anarchist opinion in order to save the life of Luis Linsuaín. But, almost unbelievably, certain sectors of international anarchism refused to accept that the "Cuban Revolution" (that is, the Cuban government) had become a totalitarian system that persecuted, imprisoned, and shot their Cuban comrades. The Cuban libertarians restated the anarchist ethical reasons for opposing the regime that persecuted them, and also supplied proof of the persecution.

But Gaona's disinformation "Clarification" document had begun to circulate in almost all of the anarchist milieus to which its authors had access, and was also being touted by agencies at the service of international marxism from Moscow to Sydney. In reply, in 1962 members of the MLCE initiated a propaganda campaign with the publication of the *Boletín de Información Libertaria (BIL)*, receiving support from *Views & Comments* in New York and the Federación Libertaria Argentina's organ, *Acción Libertaria*. The Argentine anarchists, like those in the U.S., responded from the first to the calls of the Cuban anarchists, and never deserted them in the difficult years to come.

The confusion in the anarchist camp regarding the Cuban situation was fomented by the Castro government's propaganda apparatus, which had enormous resources, talent, imagination, and great political ability. It replied to the exiled anarchists' attacks precisely in that ideological territory which marxism had manipulated so successfully during the Spanish Civil War. The international left consisted of a number of political, social, and even religious groups that constantly attacked capitalism, militarism, the ruling class, and organized religion. The entrance of the "socialist" Castro regime into this political war zone was a very effective tactic in maintaining international sympathy for the regime and for keeping it in power. This was an especially powerful tactic in combination with the Castro regime's extremely sophisticated methods of repression; and these two factors are the principal reasons for that regime's durability.

In this propaganda war, the Castro regime of course used Gaona's "Clarification" document to the fullest, even in the remotest parts of the planet, to "prove" that the anarchists' charges—which they deceitfully labeled "anti-Cuban," deliberately confusing the country with the political system—were in fact the product of ex-anarchists in the pay of the worst capitalist elements. They called the Cuban anarchists "CIA agents, go-betweens, drug traffickers, Batista supporters," and many other epithets common to marxist propaganda. But above all they circulated the DDG in all of the libertarian milieus to which they had access, in this manner creating confusion first and doubt later in regard to the MLCE.

Of course, one would have expected this maneuver. What really surprised the Cuban anarchists was the reaction to it in the anarchist world. From the beginning the Cubans had believed in the justness of their cause. After supplying proof of their persecution in Cuba and receiving the solidarity of the American and Argentinian anarchists, they assumed—erroneously as it turned out—that, given the justness of their charges against Castroism, the rest of the world's anarchists would naturally and spontaneously rally to their aid, as they had to the Spanish anarchist victims of Franco. But this didn't happen. Doubts were raised in anarchist groups in Mexico, Venezuela, Uruguay, France, and Italy. Initially, these doubts were comprehensible in relation to the revolutionary process that was coming to a head in Cuba—especially so given that the same Cuban anarchists who were now in exile and attacking Castro had initially supported the revolutionary system.

At this time, in the mid and late 1960s, there's no doubt that the DDG was doing its damage. The MLCE knew of it, but did little to combat it, assuming that no one would pay attention to such calumnies and fallacies. The MLCE strategy was to attack Castroism as the only political enemy. In hindsight, this was an error in judgment. In these years, there was a convergence in the charges made by the MLCE against Castroism and the charges made by the U.S. State Department against it. This was taken advantage of by the

Castroites who charged that the Cuban libertarians were "following the imperialist political line."

No one has ever denied the coincidence of the charges made; this was, and to a point still is, a fact. But anyone familiar with the history of anarchism and its partisans will recognize that at different times and places anarchists have made charges against governments similar to those made by the capitalist class, the Communist Party, and even the Vatican. When there's a common enemy, one makes common cause with others, no matter how little one's ideas coincide with theirs. But it's one thing to make charges similar to those of non-anarchist forces and entirely another to place oneself under their command. In the Cuban case, the Cuban anarchists always maintained their independence. As well, one should ask who opposed Castro first? It's undeniable that the Cuban anarchists opposed Castro before the U.S. government did.

While the Cuban regime's calumnies proliferated, confusion spread and the polemic escalated. Agustín Souchy's *Testimonios sobre la Revolución Cubana* and the anti-Castro *Manifiesto de los Anarquistas de Chile* circulated slowly in Latin America, and there were some defenders of the Cuban libertarian cause, including Edgar Rodrigues in Brazil and Ricardo Mestre in Mexico. Still, the *Boletin de Información Libertaria (BIL)* expressed surprise at the small amount of solidarity expressed by some anarchist sectors, and attributed it to "lack of true and exact information" about the Cuban situation. Already by 1962 the *BIL* reported a certain "declared hostility" in some anarchist media and an "incomprehension" in others.

At this time, the polemic concerning the Cuban Revolution intensified alarmingly. Writing about this useless rhetorical dispute 20 years later, Alfredo Gómez quotes Jacobo Prince (who wrote the introduction to Souchy's *Testimonios* pamphlet): "Jacobo Prince . . . in a letter of December 5, 1961 emphasized that 'the fact that the most violent attacks against the Castro regime come from reactionary sectors augments the *confusion* and makes necessary considerable *civil courage* to attack the myth of this revolution.'" It's understandable that the anarchist media suspected the enemies of Castroism, among whom one found the Cuban compañeros, but it's difficult to understand why they doubted the word of their exiled Cuban comrades, given that there was no evidence against them save the DDG, which should have been obvious to anyone reading it as a lying, malignant piece of disinformation.

The care with which anarchists had to treat the Cuban matter was well demonstrated in Venezuela and Mexico. According to Alfredo

Gómez, the Grupo Malatesta in Venezuela "in the course of a campaign for the liberation of L.M. Linsuaín [condemned to death for his attempt on Raúl Castro] . . . had to be very careful to 'clarify' and to explain exactly what the anarchists wanted . . . and to demonstrate that they weren't reactionaries." Later, in regard to *Tierra y Libertad*, the anarchist organ in Mexico, Gòmez relates that this publication "had to explain that its criticism of the Castro regime did not imply the acceptance of the pre-revolutionary structures." In both these cases, we can see that doubts and confusion prevailed in both Caracas and Mexico City. But in the end the campaign to save Linsuaín's life was successful, though he was still sentenced to 30 years imprisonment.

In Havana, in late 1961, Castro declared that he had been "a marxist-leninist [his] entire life." And other compañeros who had escaped the emerging tyranny began to arrive in Miami. Santiago Cobo César, who had occupied positions of responsibility in the Secretaría de la Federación Nacional de Transporte, one of the largest and most important unions on the island, arrived in Miami via Venezuela, where he had been given political asylum. Once in Miami, he plunged into working with the MLCE with the energy that had characterized him since his youth.

Another exile, Manuel Ferro, already of retirement age, recommenced his libertarian activism which had begun in the 1920s. Ferro was a lucid anarchist writer who had numerous international contacts, and he didn't delay in undertaking the long task, as difficult as it was fruitful, of attempting to shed some light within the shadows of incomprehension that were engulfing the libertarian world at this time in regard to Cuba.

In the company of his old Italian friend Enrico Arrigoni, and urged on by him, Ferro commenced "to write several articles about the Cuban reality" which, with the help of Arrigoni's translations, were published in the anarchist press of France, Italy, Mexico, and Argentina. According to Ferro, "In the majority of our milieus [these articles] were received with displeasure," owing to the "enthusiasm" with which the Cuban Revolution had been received in them. But in other cases anarchists rallied to the Cuban libertarian cause. *Reconstruir* ("To Reconstruct") in Buenos Aires, whose publishing house, Colectivo, fully identified with the Cuban anarchists, published all of Ferro's works.

In regard to Europe, Ferro (who signed his articles "Justo Muriel"), regularly sent his pieces to the exiled Spanish anarchist leadership, which at this time resided in Toulouse, France. His friend Federica

Montseny[4] only published three. She explained, with the cynical sincerity born of long political experience, "It's not popular to attack Castro in Europe." In reply, Ferro noted that "Neither is it popular to attack Franco in Miami."

The intellectual activity of Ferro and of Abelardo Iglesias, among other Cuban anarchists, was unceasing in the early and mid 1960s. For example, in 30 short dictums, such as the following, published in *Acción Libertaria* in Buenos Aires as "Revolución y Contrarevolución," Iglesias clarified the abysmal differences between the marxist and anarchist conceptions of revolution[5]:

> To expropriate capitalist enterprises, handing them over to the workers and technicians, THIS IS REVOLUTION.
> But to convert them into state monopolies in which the only right of the producer is to obey, THIS IS COUNTER-REVOLUTION.

Also in these years the exiled Cubans made their first contacts with the long-established Italian-American anarchists, almost all of whom were already retired in Tampa and Miami. These elderly militants sustained a publication in New York called *L'Adunata dei Refrattari* ("The Reunion of the Refractory") which in these years dedicated itself to defending Castroism or the Cuban Revolution, since to its editors, the same as to the government in Havana, the two were identical. This confusion persisted, and a debate ensued not only with the MLCE but also with the Libertarian League.

Ferro and Arrigoni began a campaign in Italy itself, with the idea of taking the bull by the horns. They turned to the most important

---

4. Montseny was a lifelong anarchist activist and had been one of the anarchist (CNT) ministers in the Largo Caballero coalition government during the Spanish Civil War.

5. Russ Blackwell translated and published this piece in the December 1961 issue of *Views & Comments*. The same issue contained an article on four imprisoned Cuban anarchists. It stated: "Luis M. Linsuaín, provincial secretary of the food workers union . . . [is being] held incommunicado in Santiago de Cuba . . . [allegedly for] plotting to kill Raúl Castro . . . Today he languishes in prison because he opposed the Stalinist takeover of his union. Aquiles Iglesias . . . [is] a qualified agronomist . . . [who] in exile during the Batista tyranny . . . from Mexico helped organize a revolutionary expedition to Cuba. He is now in prison and is reported to have received a very long term sentence. José Aceña . . . [who] participate[d] actively in the struggle against Batista . . . was seized in August [1961] and he is still held incommunicado. Sandalio Torres, a libertarian sympathizer, is a construction worker . . . [He] fought in the underground against Batista. He was jailed last October . . . and is now held in Pinar del Río. Four times he has faced the firing squad to force a 'confession' implicating others."

Italian anarchist periodical, *Umanita Nova* ("New Humanity"), the official publication of the Federazione Anarchica Italiana, with the idea of counterbalancing the undeniable influence of *L'Adunata* in the Italian-American anarchist community, and more especially of responding to a series of pro-Cuban Revolution articles published in that weekly by Armando Borghi. *Umanita Nova* refused to publish Ferro's articles (translated by Arrigoni), saying that they didn't want to create a polemic. At that point Arrigoni accused them of being in the pay of the Communists, and they eventually published Ferro's responses to Borghi. A few months later, Borghi—ignoring the points raised by Ferro—published a new defense of Castroism in *L'Adunata*, but *Umanita Nova* refused to publish Ferro's response to it.

In Cuba at this time there were still a few anarchists suffering in silence the despotism of the Castro regime. Guerra, Sierra, and Salinas, who were all elderly veterans of the struggles of the 1920s and 1930s, were abandoned to their fate despite the efforts of their compañeros in exile to aid them in obtaining the necessities of life. The first two of these had signed Gaona's "Clarification" document against their will, as they admitted in private. Salinas, who had refused to be an accomplice to this crime, was forced by the government to go into a type of internal exile in Santiago de las Vegas, from which place he would later go into actual exile in Miami. Another veteran anarchist, Modesto Barbeito, would die shortly, a victim of frustration and ill health.

During these years there were many anarchists imprisoned for "counter-revolutionary activities," such as Antonio Dagas, a Spaniard who belonged to the CNT delegation in Cuba, who was imprisoned in the sinister La Cabaña prison in Havana.[6] Alberto García, the Secretary of the Federación de Trabajadores Médicos, was condemned to 30 years imprisonment. Sandalio Torres, accused of "conspiracy against the powers of the state," was sentenced to 10 years in prison for refusing to make false conspiracy charges against other anarchists.

Another member of the CNT delegation among the anarchists in Cuba was Salvador García, who eventually obtained asylum in Mexico. Upon his arrival, he made contact with other exiled Spaniards, such as Ricardo Mestre, Fidel Miró, Domingo Rojas, Ismael Viadu, and Marcos Alcón, all of whom sympathized with the MLCE. After his

---

6. La Cabaña is a 400-year-old Spanish fort at the entrance of Havana Bay. It was used in colonial times as a jail and place of execution. This is the prison which has the famous "paredón," or "big wall," where the executions of the first days of the revolution took place.

arrival, *Tierra y Libertad* published the testimony of García, which not only affirmed that persecution of libertarians was taking place in Cuba, but also endorsed the opinions of the MLCE. Later, in 1962, the always-supportive *Reconstruir* would publish García's account in Argentina.

At about the same time, the Comité Pro-Libertarios Presos (Committee for Libertarian Prisoners) was created in Miami to collect funds to help alleviate the hardships of the compañeros suffering in Castro's prisons.

In the middle of 1963, Abelardo Iglesias finished writing a booklet of nearly 100 pages titled *Revolución y dictadura en Cuba* ("Revolution and Dictatorship in Cuba"), which with a prologue by Jacobo Prince was published in Buenos Aires in October. Iglesias, as Prince noted, had written with characteristic sincerity a document "with the authority of exemplary militance over a period of 30 years, and which sees [the Cuban] people subjected to a new dictatorship." *Revolución y dictadura*, a calm denunciation of Castro, offered a description of Cuban society beneath the "revolutionary" regime. It ended with some conclusions about the subordination of Cuban foreign policy to the Kremlin, and about what the author considered "the correct tactic" against the new dictatorship: "revolutionary war."

Meanwhile in New York in 1964, the Libertarian League under Sam Dolgoff's leadership was continuing its propaganda campaign against the Castro government, and also organizing public demonstrations against it. At this time, a controversy arose between Dolgoff and Dave Dellinger, the pacifist writer, upon Dellinger's return from Cuba after the May Day celebrations in Havana (the trip being paid for by the Castro regime)—with, of course, the obligatory military parades, Soviet slogans, and *The International* as background music.

Following his return, Dellinger wrote a pro-Castro piece which was published in the "anarcho-pacifist" magazine, *Liberation,* edited by David Wieck. Members of the Libertarian League and some Cuban anarchists publicly protested in front of *Liberation's* editorial offices, accusing Dellinger and Wieck of being "apologists for the Castro regime." Long-time American anarchist Mike Hargis recalls, "While most of the left in the U.S., including some erstwhile anarchists, like the pacifists David Thoreau Wieck and David Dellinger, joined in denunciation of the MLCE (Cuban Libertarian Movement in Exile) as CIA stooges, the Libertarian League and the IWW came to their defense publishing the statements and manifestos of the MLCE in *Views & Comments* and publicly challenging Castro's leftist apologists for their willful blindness."

That blindness allowed Castro's persecution of Cuba's anarchists to go unchallenged by foreign leftists, including anarchists. The persecution of the anarchists was intense in the 1961–1972 period. It's difficult to know exactly how many libertarians were jailed, for as little as a few days or over 20 years, as in the case of Cuco Sánchez, a baker from the city of Holguin in Oriente Province, who was imprisoned for many long years in the Cárcel de Boniato in Santiago de Cuba. Another who suffered was the already elderly Jesús Iglesias (no relation to Abelardo) who was sentenced to 20 years and served time on the Isle of Pines and in the Combinado del Este prison near Havana. When he was released he had no family and no place to live. He eventually moved to Guanabacoa, where he died in poverty. At present—because the anarchist movement was relatively weak when Castro came to power, and because a great many Cuban anarchists fled into exile—there are no more than 400 anarchists left in Cuba, of whom perhaps 100 were political prisoners at one time or another.

At any rate, at the beginning of 1965 at a congress of the Federación Anarquista Uruguaya (FAU) celebrated in Montevideo, the growing fractionalization of the Southern Cone anarchists in regard to Cuba became clear. A majority of the members of the FAU, with some exceptions such as Luce Fabbri,[7] didn't hide their sympathies for the Castro regime. For their part the Argentine delegation, invited to represent the Federación Libertaria Argentina, opposed this position. This polemic ended by splitting the FAU into pro- and anti-Castro factions, with the pro-Castro majority—according to the article "Living My Life," by Luce Fabbri, published years later in the Italian anarchist review, *Rivista Anarchica*—ending up either in exile in Sweden or in the ranks of the urban guerrilla group, the Tupamaros. This group achieved nothing positive. It provoked the downfall of Uruguay's democratic government and its replacement by a military regime, while at the same time providing that regime with the perfect pretext for the institution of massive repression, extra-judicial executions, and routine torture of political prisoners.[8]

---

7. Daughter of Luigi Fabbri, and a noted anarchist writer in her own right.

8. For a gut-wrenching depiction of the brutality of this struggle, see the Costa-Gavras film, *State of Siege*. For an anarchist analysis of the question of terrorism and urban guerrilla warfare, see the pamphlet, *You Can't Blow Up a Social Relationship: The Anarchist Case Against Terrorism*, by anonymous Australian anarchists, published by See Sharp Press. See also, *Bourgeois Influences on Anarchism*, by Luigi Fabbri, which is now published by Left Bank Distribution in the U.S. The original Spanish-language version is available as *Influencias burguesas sobre el anarquismo* from Ediciones Antorcha in Mexico City. —CB

In view of the confusion surrounding the Cuban situation among the world's anarchists, the Federazione Anarchica Italiana organized a conference in Bologna to clarify things; this conference was held from March 27 through March 29, 1965, and a delegate from the MLCE was invited to present the position of the Cuban libertarians. The Cubans collected funds and sent Abelardo Iglesias as their representative, because Iglesias had experience with this type of discussion and was well able to express the MLCE's viewpoint.

After visiting in Toulouse and Paris with other veterans of the Spanish Revolution, Iglesias traveled to Bologna where he successfully presented the MLCE's arguments against Castro. The Federazione Anarchica Italiana (FAIT) energetically condemned Castroism—noting that Castro had substituted vassalage to the Soviet Union in place of vassalage to the United States—and offered the MLCE its full support in the struggle against Castro-Communism. It also pledged to support the campaign against the political executions taking place in Cuba.[9] The congress ended by calling for all of the Italian anarchist periodicals—*Umanita Nova, L'Agitazione del Sud, Semo Anarchico, Volanta*, and others—to publish its accords. In addition to the FAIT, the Federación Libertaria Argentina, the Federación Libertaria Mexicana, the Libertarian League (U.S.), the Anarchist Federation of London, the Sveriges Arbetares Central-Organisation (Swedish Central Workers' Organization—SAC), and the Movimiento Libertario Español signed the accords.

After the Bologna congress, Iglesias returned to Toulouse where he presented the MLCE position at the congress of the French Anarchist Federation. That congress condemned the "marxist-leninist counter-revolution" that had subverted the Cuban Revolution, denouncing the Castro regime as being as bad as a fascist dictatorship or one in the pay of the U.S. The French federation promised support for the anarchists in Cuban jails and to let French working people know about the fate of their Cuban brothers in the pages of the most important French anarchist paper, *Le Monde Libertaire*.

Upon returning to the U.S., it appeared that Iglesias had not only won the long and vitriolic debate with Castro's sympathizers, but had

---

9. Only the Castro regime knows how many prisoners it's shot. Nevertheless, one can make certain conjectures. At the very least, thousands of political prisoners died in Castro's jails and prisons. According to historian Juan Clark, "Shootings, beatings, hunger strikes, accidents during forced labor . . . suicides . . . the death penalty for "counter-revolutionary" crimes and crimes "against state security—and such sentences are still being handed down—claimed at least tens of thousands of lives [since Castro came to power]."

also managed to prod almost all of the federations and libertarian groups in Europe and Latin America into condemning the system imposed by Castro—a double victory. This wasn't the case. The Castroite penetration of anarchist milieus—or better, the self-deception of a great many in those milieus—had established the idea of the necessity of a "permanent revolution" in Latin America and Africa. Any criticism of the Castro regime was seen as a criticism of this new political adventure emanating from Havana, which was bringing to a head the world socialist revolution. To this totalitarian mindset, anyone who wasn't behind Castroism and third-worldism was an enemy of the people and of humanity. Sadly, the majority of anarchist groups in Europe and in Latin America (as in Uruguay, Peru, Chile, and Venezuela) passed over into the camp of the Cuban Revolution—now *always* capitalized—and forgot about the MLCE and the Cuban anarchists.

The factionalism the marxists hoped to foment (through the DDG document and other pieces of disinformation) had come to pass. According to Alfredo Gómez, "The Cuban anarchists . . . have lived in impressive solitude, abandoned . . . by the anarchists of the rest of the world who identify themselves with the Cuban Communist Party." But despite all, the Cuban anarchists in the MLCE continued their campaigns for the political prisoners in Cuban jails and against the Castro regime.

In 1967, Marcelo Salinas, already in his late 70s and fatigued by his sufferings on the island, arrived in Miami. Salinas could have signed the DDG and thus ensured himself an honored place as a leading intellectual in Castro's Cuba. But he refused to sign, and instead chose at his advanced age to go into exile, an exile among rightist and conservative elements who had no appreciation of him or his works. But once in exile he continued his libertarian efforts by writing articles for the anarchist press and by speaking at conferences.

He was already known abroad through his extensive personal correspondence of 50 years, and through writing for *Reconstruir* in Buenos Aires. Once in exile, his activities complemented those of Ferro and Iglesias. He continued his work until his death in 1976 at the age of 87. With the passing of Marcelo Salinas, the MLCE not only lost a dedicated comrade who had been active in the anarchist movement for 70 years, but Cuba lost in this thin figure one of the most well-rounded intellectuals of his generation. He was a dramatist, poet, novelist, essayist, and story teller; in sum, he was an enlightened autodidact who was an intellectual force of the first order both inside and outside of Cuba.

The chaotic decade of the 1960s was coming to its close. In 1968, Herbert Marcuse in Berkeley preached a marxism close to anarchism, and in Boston Noam Chomsky criticized all the horrors of the North American state; in Paris, the new French philosophers attacked Marx, and in the same city in May of that year a general strike broke out in which students, using anarchist slogans and the black flag, took part; American youths at this time dedicated themselves to stopping the Vietnam War, avoiding the draft (not necessarily in that order), and opening themselves to government repression through the use of illegal drugs; the U.S. was caught up in internal strife, both racial and political; the USSR invaded Czechoslovakia to avoid the kind of marxism Marcuse was preaching in Berkeley; simultaneously in Havana Castro applauded this tragic, totalitarian maneuver; and in China, Mao instituted the violent and despotic "cultural revolution." It was in the latter part of this year that the Federazione Anarchica Italiana called an International Congress of Anarchist Federations.

Known as the Congress of Carrara, it was held from August 30 to September 8, and was widely covered not only by the anarchist media but by the world media. This conference included representatives from virtually all of the Western European countries as well as delegations of Mexicans and exiled Bulgarians. The Swedish SAC, the Centre Internationale pour Recherches sur L'Anarchisme (a Swiss anarchist research group) and the Asociación Internacional de los Trabajadores (the anarcho-syndicalist international) participated as observers. This was one of the largest anarchist conferences held in over half a century.

Due to lack of funds, the MLCE was unable to send a delegate, and therefore asked Domingo Rojas, from Mexico, to represent the Cuban anarchists at the conference. The congress hammered out eight points of agreement, and the most discussed was point 3, on the relationship of anarchism and marxism in the Russian, Spanish, and Cuban revolutions.

The conferees didn't have doubts about the sinister actions of the marxists in Russia and Spain, but Cuba was a different matter. With the backdrop of the libertarian disasters in Russia and Spain, the conferees declared that the Castro system was indeed "a dictatorship . . . a satellite of the USSR," etc. But they then concluded with a paragraph that was as out of place as it was contradictory: "Cuba is a more permeable country to the theories . . . of a type of libertarian communism unlike that of the USSR and its satellite countries." In other words, Cuban "scientific socialism" was a different case—though they didn't explain why—and there was therefore hope of penetrating the Castro regime in order to get it to modify its statist, totalitarian policies, and to adopt in their place anarchist principles in accord with liberty and justice.

Analyzing this accord 30 years later, it seems pathetic, even considering the time in which it was written. The world's anarchists had lost their perspective on Cuba. The words of this document are an indication of how the Castro regime was winning the propaganda battle on the left with its false "revolutionary" postulates and slogans; it also clearly demonstrates the penetration of Castroite propaganda in the anarchist world in regard to the MLCE. The anarchist media in Europe and Latin America supported the Cuban regime more each day as they abandoned their Cuban compañeros, the victims of that regime.[10] To this day, with almost no exceptions, they have never publicly admitted this mistake.

It's true that many anarchists in Europe and Latin America were aware of the nature of Castro's dictatorship over the Cuban people and of Castro's persecution of Cuba's anarchists. But it's also true that, with the sole exception of *Umanita Nova*'s publication of Ferro's response to Borghi (and that only under pressure), not a single anarchist periodical in Europe, and very few in Latin America, published a single article acknowledging—much less condemning—Castro's dictatorship and political persecutions.

By 1970 the MLCE knew that it had lost the battle. Even though the Cuban anarchists kept up the propaganda fight, they knew they were speaking to the deaf. The bitter words of Abelardo Iglesias in *BIL* in 1970 are explicit: "those who pick up the Communist accusations don't hesitate in accusing us of being in the service of reaction. [These include] *Adunata de Refrattari* . . . F[ederación] A[narquista] U[ruguaya] . . . Federazione Anarchica Italiana and its periodical, *Umanita Nova* . . . Daniel Cohn-Bendit, etc." Iglesias recounted that at Carrara Cohn-Bendit "accused the MLCE of being 'financed by the CIA.'" In another article published later, Alfredo Gómez mentioned that *Le Monde Libertaire*, the publication of the Federacion Anarchiste Francaise, had published a piece mentioning all current dictatorships —except that of Cuba. This was "as if the French comrades" con-

---

10. The Cuban anarchists weren't totally abandoned. They still had supporters, including Jacobo Prince, Agustín Souchy, Gustavo Leval, Frank Mintz, Luce Fabbri, E. Cressatti, Edgar Rodrigues, Juan Campá, Fidel Miró, Ricardo Mestre, Marcos Alcón, Sam Dolgoff, Progreso Alfarache, Cipriano Mera, Luis Mercier, Ilario Margarita, Helmut Rüdinger, and some anarchist organizations such as the Federación Anarquista Argentina, Federación Anarquista Mexicana, CNT Mexicana, and the Libertarian League

sidered Cuba an exception and also "considered the Cuban anarchists second-class anarchists, undeserving of their solidarity."

Even in 1975 there still remained much mistrust of Cuba's libertarians in the anarchist world. At the end of that year, the well-designed anarchist magazine *Comunidad* ("Community"), published in Stockholm by refugees (primarily Uruguayans) from the dictatorships in South America's Southern Cone, printed an article titled, "Libertarian Presence in Latin America," which was later republished in the Spanish anarchist magazine, *Bicicleta* ("Bicycle") in a special edition dedicated to "Anarchism Throughout the World." In reference to the Cuban anarchists, the article's authors stated that the MLCE was composed of "mere anti-Communists," and that its positions were "clearly regressive." This charge was so ridiculous that the MLCE sent *Bicicleta* a reply to it partially in jest. This response was originally published in *BIL* and stated, in part: "In regard to our 'clearly regressive positions,' these have always consisted of opposition to the tyrant of the day, be they in Cuba or anywhere else, no matter what their stripe . . . [no matter] what religion they profess or what political dogma they follow." Curiously, *Bicliceta* never published the MLCE reply despite the fact that its special edition was headed by the statement that it was intended to "stir up debate . . . to open up debate."

The accusations in the *Comunidad/Bicicleta* article were typical. The charge in those days was that the MLCE was a reactionary organization with no program beyond anti-Communism. No mention was ever made about *why* Cuba's anarchists were in exile, and this charge fit neatly with Castro's propaganda which ceaselessly repeated that all of the "counter-revolutionary sectors in Miami" were owned by the capitalists and were engaging in such things as drug trafficking and white slavery. Anyone familiar with the situation would have known that these were outrageous slanders against the MLCE, but anyone depending upon the world's anarchist press for information about Cuba wouldn't have known it.

It wasn't until 1976 that the atmosphere of suspicion and distrust of the MLCE began to dissipate, with the publication of *The Cuban Revolution: A Critical Perspective*, by Sam Dolgoff. This book was well distributed in the English-speaking world, from London to Sydney, and had a demolishing impact among the left in general and anarchists in particular. It was the must cutting critique Castroism had received in these years of "revolutionary" adventurism in Latin America, and was the decisive factor in the change in attitude toward the MLCE within world anarchism. The book succeeded beyond the hopes of its author, and was translated into Spanish and later into Swedish. Dolgoff subsequently declared, "I never received a cent for these printings, but I felt happy to be able to propagate my opinions about the MLCE and its struggle against Castro in this book."

At the end of 1979, in the first post-Franco years in Spain, when the anarchist Confederación Nacional del Trabajo/Asociación Internacional de los Trabajadores (CNT/AIT) could again begin to operate without being persecuted by the government, a celebratory congress was called in Madrid. An MLCE delegate was invited to participate, and he was recognized by a majority of those present, including almost all of the foreign representatives. At this point the MLCE, which at the time was primarily concerned with bettering relations with other sectors of international anarchism, renewed its fraternal ties with the AIT.

A few months later, the Spanish periodical *Bicicleta*, which in those years was printing anarchist materials, published part of the previously quoted piece by Alfredo Gómez, "The Cuban Anarchists, or the Bad Conscience of Anarchism." This piece was later reprinted by the exiled Bulgarian anarchists in their organ, *IZTOK*, in Paris, and was still later reprinted by the new magazine of the MLCE in Miami, *Guángara Libertaria*, in the summer 1981 issue. (See below.) Iglesias followed with an explicatory article in the autumn issue, which further delineated the position of the MLCE in regard to Castro, and above all addressed the anarchist world of the period. He quoted Progreso Alfarache Arrabal (a Spanish anarchist member of the CNT who had fled to Mexico and was member of the editorial group producing *Tierra y Libertad*). Alfarache commented on the actions and attitudes of many anarchists: "In the Cuban case, the keen instinct for liberty, which is the essence of anarchism, has failed lamentably." One can well regard this article by Iglesias as the termination of this long and damaging affair.

But there were also changes in the world which were affecting the anarchists. A new antiauthoritarian world view had begun to take hold in the 1970s, and in the 1980s Castroism came to be seen by anarchists as it really was (and is)—a self-aggrandizing dictatorship that didn't represent its people. Although a long but sure repudiation of the Castro regime had begun among the world's anarchists, it was already very late. The Cuban anarchists had been the victims of prejudice and defamation in the anarchist world, in addition to being exiled, thrown in jail, and being consigned to a shadowy solitude.

Despite everything, the Cuban anarchists launched their new quarterly magazine, *Guángara Libertaria*, in November 1979. It was published in Miami, and its first issue appeared in January 1980. An average issue consisted of 32 8.5"X11" pages printed in black ink on newsprint. *Guángara* superseded the two existing Cuban anarchist publications, the *BIL* and *El Gastronómico*, which were modest bulletins with limited circulation. *Guángara* was designed to have broader appeal to and wider circulation among the Cuban exile community. This new publication was financed by its staff, subscribers, and members of the MLCE.

The name had been suggested by Abelardo Iglesias, who noted that "for Cubans, it means noise, disorder, and a rough joke. Definitively, *bronca* (a coarse joke), *bulla* (a loud argument), and *guángara* can be taken as synonyms for chaos and disorder." In keeping with this anarchistic spirit, the position of "director" (in effect, managing editor) was abolished and *Guángara* was collectively managed and edited. The editorial collective included Santiago Cobo, Omar Dieguez, Luis Dulzaides, Frank Fernández, and Casto Moscú. The administrative aspects were handled by a collective including José R. Álvarez, Agustín Castro, Manuel Gonzalez, and Aristides Vazquez.[11]

The content at this time consisted of articles written by the editorial staff as well as those submitted by readers (primarily Cuban and Spanish anarchists) spread throughout the anarchist diaspora in the Americas. Translations from English-language anarchist periodicals also appeared. *Guángara* included a book review section (edited by Manuel Ferro), portraits of historical anarchist figures, and news and opinion about events in Cuba and in the exile community. During these first years of its existence, *Guángara* had a press run of 1000 copies and was distributed only in Miami, though it had about 100 subscribers scattered around the globe.

Given the place where the magazine was published, Miami—home base of the extreme right-wing Cuban exile community—*Guángara*'s editors knew from the start that they'd have to be careful about how the magazine presented itself. There was a very real danger of physical violence from right-wing elements, and both local and federal authorities were, of course, keeping them under observation. So, for the first few years *Guángara* was fairly muted in its advocacy of anarchism, billing itself in its subtitle as "The Review of Eclectic Libertarian Thought." It also ran articles by nonanarchists, including social democrats, though of course all such articles still fell in the

---

11. As in so many other collectives, the work and responsibility were not evenly distributed at *Guángara*, and the author of this book, Frank Fernández, served as *de facto* editor throughout almost the entire length of *Guángara*'s existence. —CB

broad "progressive" vein. All of this led some purist types to charge that *Guángara* was more "literary" than libertarian.

At about the time of *Guángara*'s appearance in early 1980, Miami was shaken by demonstrations following the occupation of the Peruvian embassy in Havana by Cubans seeking asylum. The MLCE anarchists in Miami participated actively in these demonstrations, while showing their colors, and they organized some of these demonstrations against the Castro dictatorship.

The first signs of an explosion occurred in the early morning hours of April 4, 1980, when a small group of Cubans entered the Peruvian embassy in Havana in search of political asylum. The Peruvian government refused to hand the asylum seekers over to the Cuban government, and in response the Cuban regime recalled the guards watching over the embassy. Then, with the guards withdrawn, a multitude of more than 10,000 people tried to seek asylum at that same embassy.

Comprehending the danger involved in this type of protest, and that it could quickly spread, the authorities decided, after a speech by the maximum leader, to permit anyone who wanted to exit the island to do so. Despite the oppressive omnipresence of the government and the willingness of many government supporters to resort to violence, in a few weeks an exodus of gigantic proportions took form. More than a quarter of a million Cubans left their homeland on boats supplied by Cuban exiles in Miami. This spectacle would have international repercussions.

The communications media of the entire world witnessed the largest human stampede in the history of the Americas, a stampede of political (and economic) refugees. This spectacle was a public relations disaster for the Castro regime, despite its skillful disinformation efforts.

Following the Mariel "boatlift," *Guángara* was reinforced by a number of intellectuals who escaped Cuba via Mariel, among them writers such as Benjamín Ferrera, Enrique G. Morató, Miguel A. Sánchez, and the Afro-Cuban poet, Esteban Luis Cárdenas. This helped to create what was in effect a new *Guángara* collective, which included writers, essayists, historians, and poets, individuals such as Pedro Leyva, Angel Aparicio Laurencio, Benito García, Ricardo Pareja, and Sergio Magarolas, among others.

At about the same time, and at Sam Dolgoff's suggestion, *Guángara* incorporated as a nonprofit under the name International Society for Historical & Social Studies (ISHSS). Various members of the MLCE served on the Society's board. The advantages of this set up were that it allowed *Guángara* to receive tax-deductible donations and also allowed it to mail its issues at minimal cost within the U.S. Following the ISHSS incorporation, *Guángara* increased its press run to 3000 copies. This made it one of the largest-circulation anarchist periodicals—perhaps *the* largest—in the U.S.; and it was the only one published in Spanish. During this period of growth, *Guángara* began to publish translations from French and Italian anarchist publications, and also began to be better received in Miami.

Feeling more confident, *Guángara*'s collective started publishing more explicitly anarchist materials, and moved beyond attacking Castro; *Guángara* began to also publish attacks on the reactionary exile community and upon the U.S. government. The attacks on the far-right exile leadership focused upon its lack of political imagination, its religious and/or pseudo-democratic orientation, and its very mistaken political and social positions, often based on disinformation planted by Castro's propaganda apparatus. (The purpose of this disinformation was to help ensure that no viable—that is, democratic and antiauthoritarian—opposition would emerge in Miami, and so that Castro could thus continue to present the Cuban people with the false choice of his regime or the extremely reactionary Cuban exile leadership.)

By the autumn of 1985, *Guángara* had a number of new international correspondents: Stephan Baciu in Hawaii, Ricardo Mestre in Mexico, Cosme Paules in Chile, Abraham Guillén in Spain, M.A. Sánchez in New York, and Victor García in Caracas. Both García and Guillén were well known among the Spanish anarchists, and their collaboration gave *Guángara* the international dimension that the MLCE had always sought.

In 1986 the collective produced a large special edition, and by 1987 *Guángara*'s circulation had increased to 5000 copies, making it the largest-circulation anarchist periodical in the U.S. The quality of both its writing and its graphic presentation had improved; and two new writers, Maria Teresa Fernández and Lucy Ibrahim, contributed both translations and poems. *Guángara* changed its subtitle that year to "A Cry of Liberty in Black & White"; in 1990, it changed it again to "From Liberty, for Liberty"

The downfall of the USSR and its long-overdue relegation to the "dustbin of history" was received with jubilation by *Guángara*'s collective and the rest of the MLCE, and *Guángara* published an editorial predicting the swift downfall of Castro. (Of course, *Guángara* was mistaken about this, but it was hardly alone; such predictions were common in the days following the fall of Castro's patron, the USSR.)

In 1992, *Guángara* published its 50th edition. It included an inventory in which it noted that *Guángara* had published over 225,000 copies. But by this time *Guángara*'s all-volunteer, entirely unpaid staff was growing weary, and the fall 1992 issue was *Guángara*'s final edition.

It would be an exaggeration to say that *Guángara* convinced half the world of the evil of Castro's regime. It would equally be an exaggeration to say that it destroyed the ideological base of Castroism. But it would be fair to say that *Guángara* breached the bulwarks of paid anti-Communism in the exile community, and that it reclaimed the right to disagree. It would also be fair to say that it opened the eyes of many who labored under the burden of pro-Castro, stalinist suppositions.

In the end, one of the most telling indications of the success of *Guángara* was that it published 54 issues over 13 years, without ever having a cover price or being sold on the newsstand. It was always free to anyone who asked for it, and it was supported solely by the contributions of its collective, its subscribers, and its MLCE supporters.

Those who worked on *Guángara* continue to pursue other projects, such as writing books and contributing to other anarchist publications.

◆ ◆ ◆

As one can appreciate, Cuba's anarchists have survived all types of persecutions from the state, instigated by the monied classes and the Cuban Communist Party. It should be equally clear that their ideas were for many years the majority viewpoint within the Cuban workers' movement; they resisted Spanish colonialism, U.S. intervention, the sugar and tobacco magnates, the hacendados and plantation owners, capitalist industrialists, and the first and second republics—and finally the most despotic, totalitarian regime Cuba has ever known.

In their long history spanning more than a century, Cuba's anarchists—those who had carried the banners, the writers, the theoreticians, the orators, the union activists, the propagandists, and even the last of the militants—made blunders and errors, which we must admit and accept. But we can be sure that they maintained the spirit of disinterested struggle for the good of Cuba and its people. Those who survive today are the inheritors of a long tradition of liberty and justice, united by the confidence that this new century will bring the dawn of a better world, a world in which their ideas will finally be put into practice.

6

Reality & Reflection

The now obvious socioeconomic failure of the Cuban revolution could not have been appreciated before the mid 1970s. During the 1960s, Cuba had sufficient monetary reserves to hide this failure: international credits, cash on hand, foreign currency, and exportable agricultural production (primarily sugar and tobacco). These economic riches, inherited from the now-defunct capitalist system, maintained the Castro regime during the first "socialist" decade, the start of which had been officially announced in 1961.

The projects and policies instituted in these first years of economic adventurism, "revolutionary" inefficiency, and failed social attempts were all based in "scientific socialism," political, social, and economic centralism, and state control of all of the island's economic activities, including all but the smallest agricultural, industrial, service, and distribution businesses. The revolutionary course in these days was based in—or at least was said to be based in—the leninist concept of "democratic centralism," in which the entire socioeconomic life of Cuba was in the hands of the Partido Comunista Cubano; and, as was the custom in the European marxist models, the direction and supervision of all of the powers emanating from the state were made the responsibility of the Political Bureau and Executive Committee of the PCC, and Fidel Castro as First Secretary of the Party.

The first and most essential project chosen by the new socialist state was the rapid substitution of a gigantic project of industrial growth and agricultural diversification to replace the cultivation of sugarcane as Cuba's economic mainstay—a monoculture which had sustained the Cuban economy since the beginning of the 19th century. With diplomatic and commercial relations with the U.S. broken, and with the U.S. economic blockade in place, this new economic direction would make it very difficult to return to the old politico-economic system. Preventing this return was precisely the aim of the Castro regime.

While this change in the economic system was taking place, the Castro government moved to establish closer ties with the Soviet

Union, a country with which Cuba had maintained diplomatic and commercial relations since 1933. So, Cuba not only made a 180 degree turn economically, it made a similar turn politically, with the USSR assuming the dominating role formerly played by the USA for almost seven decades.

Cuba's workers and campesinos didn't benefit much from this transition from capitalism to leninism, nor from the substitution of the USSR for the USA as political master. In fact, this transition brought with it some of the worst labor abuses since the darkest days of Spanish colonialism.

The regime instituted "voluntary" hours of additional work, with the stated purpose of building "socialism," a system which no one appeared to understand. To these extra hours, "Red Sundays" were added—"voluntary" days of (of course) unpaid work by students. At this time, one of the most popular slogans, repeated daily, was that of "making unemployment disappear"; and with all of these "voluntary" days and hours of unpaid work, the regime certainly succeeded in achieving that goal. But, curiously, this isn't one of the achievements touted as a triumph of Castro's first few years in power.

At the same time that these economic plans were being implemented, shortages began to appear in the necessities of daily life, and the government instituted rationing. Each citizen had a monthly allotment of food and clothing—an allotment the government couldn't always supply. This rapidly led to protests, but these protests were quashed by the Committees for the Defense of the Revolution and by the state security apparatus. The protests, however, were clearly an alarm bell, and the government fast realized that its new economic measures, planned and instituted so quickly, had become a social and economic disaster. So, it changed course again in an even more marxist direction.

The government then implemented Ernesto Guevara's old proposals to complete the "collectivization of the means of production" and to create a system which at all costs would avoid material incentives, a system that would obligate the Cubans to become "new human beings"—honest, egalitarian, nonegotistical, and above all in possession of a "superior revolutionary consciousness" and thus willing to sacrifice everything for the construction of a socialist society. So, in 1968, the government, as part of a "revolutionary offensive," seized all the remaining small businesses in Cuba for the purpose of liquidating forever the hated "petit bourgeoisie" who still stubbornly persisted in creating personal wealth. Despite these measures which not only didn't improve things, but made them worse, the Castro regime and its policies could still count on the backing of many of those at the bottom of the social pyramid.

Things began to change dramatically after the failure of the touted "10 million ton sugar crop" campaign in 1970. This agro-industrial operation involved the unprecedented militarization of the labor force for the sowing, cutting, and milling of sugar, and also the slashing and burning of woods and other unspoiled natural areas in order to increase the area for the planting of sugarcane. This process, which involved cutting down large number of trees and the diversion of farm fields and pasture land to sugar production, caused long-lasting and perhaps irreparable damage to Cuba's natural environment. This process was so gigantic that it even affected rainfall and drainage patterns. Perhaps the most notable effect of this was the siltation and salinization of Cuba's rivers and reservoirs. (Unfortunately, this lack of concern for Cuba's natural environment persists to this day.) But despite these draconian and environmentally disastrous measures, the goal of a 10 million ton sugar harvest wasn't even approached.

After this dramatic failure, the USSR began to realize that the attempted rapid industrialization of the island and the reorganization of agriculture had been monumental errors. As Cuba's primary outlet for its products, the USSR "suggested" that the Castro regime return to the old methods of planting, harvesting, and milling sugar. But the damage was done. Future sugar harvest yields were all below what had been projected, and the island atrophied economically for almost a decade—as was predictable, given that Cuba's workers had wasted almost a full year on Castro's impossible "10 million ton" project. Everyone could see that this scheme was both an economic and an ecological disaster, and the Cuban people began to distance themselves from the government.

Of course the Soviet bureaucracy in Moscow understood that the Cuban agricultural project wasn't producing adequate dividends, and as is natural in these sorts of affairs, it decided to up the ante. It drastically increased aid to the Cuban government beginning in 1971. This aid didn't consist of ICBMs or nuclear weapons; it consisted of massive amounts of development aid and commercial subsidies. The annual subsidy in the years 1961–1970 averaged $327 million (over $1.5 billion yearly in 2001 dollars), and in the decade 1971–1980 averaged $1.573 billion per year (over $5 billion today).

But despite this massive aid from the Soviet Union, popular discontent grew in Cuba in a manner unexpected by the guardians of the system. Public disillusionment with the false promises of the revolution's leaders grew rapidly during the 1970s, resulting in increased repression, jailings, and exiles.

To get a better idea of the extent of the repression in these years, one should note that new penal facilities were built in every single province throughout the length of the island. These consisted of prisons, jails, forced labor (one could fairly call them "concentration") camps, and prison farms. Prisoners were used to construct all of these. In 1984 there were 144 jails and prisons throughout the island holding tens of thousands of inmates, both common and political prisoners. The last data available indicate that there were 168 Cuban prisons in 1988 holding common prisoners (including those caught attempting currency transactions involving U.S. dollars), political prisoners, and those who had attempted to escape the island. In those years, the number of prisons and the number of prisoners in Cuba increased in an almost Malthusian manner.

The Cuban people weren't the only ones suffering from Castro's policies at this time; the people of Latin America and Africa were, too. In accord with the policy of "national liberation," the Castro regime supported guerrilla movements—both urban and rural—in almost all of the countries south of the Rio Grande. These movements ran head on into an iron determination by the U.S. government to keep control of the countries in its sphere of influence. This resulted in short order in the Castro-backed insurgents provoking the creation of military dictatorships (backed, of course, by the CIA), a gang of uniformed gorillas who dedicated themselves to kidnappings, "disappearances," rape, robbery, torture, and murder—directed as much against innocent civilians as against their guerrilla enemies. Literally hundreds of thousands of people died as a result in countries such as Guatemala, El Salvador, Argentina, and Colombia.

In Africa, the Cuban regime intervened militarily in several countries, most notably Ethiopia (on the side of the murderously repressive, marxist-leninist Dergue government, in its attempts to suppress the independence movements in Tigre and Eritrea) and Angola. Over a period of more than a decade, Cuba sent hundreds of thousands of soldiers to fight in African campaigns, in the above-mentioned countries and also in others, such as Algeria, the Congo, and Sudan; the Cuban troops found themselves involved in uprisings, coups d'etat, civil wars, tribal conflicts, and undeclared wars. The same Cuban troops who fought against South Africa for the independence of Namibia exterminated entire villages in Angola and Ethiopia. All of this cost Cuba many millions of dollars as well as tens of thousands of military casualties.

This long history of disasters and injustice, both inside and outside of Cuba, led even those Cubans who still support the government first to doubts, then to apathy, and finally to a frustration which they themselves don't understand. All of this has led to a mass desire to escape the country. But that's a bit difficult, given that the Constitution of 1976 denies Cuba's citizens the right to freely travel abroad—or, more accurately, to flee the regime that oppresses them. This constitutional prohibition was, however, a formality, as measures denying the Cuban people that freedom had already been in force for years.

After the 1980 Mariel "boatlift," Castro's Cuba appeared to have stabilized itself at least economically, even though social tension continued. Soviet economic aid contributed notably to this economic stabilization; it increased further in the 1981–1985 period to a total of $22.658 billion, an average of $4.5 billion a year (roughly $8 billion today). This was by far the most aid Cuba had ever received throughout its history, and these huge figures graphically demonstrate the heavy involvement of Moscow in the remote Caribbean island.

Despite this massive aid, the results of the first 25 years of Castroism couldn't have been more negative. Cuba's economy was directly and massively dependent on the USSR, and its government was a dictatorship that permitted no criticism—despite the empty words of the 1976 Constitution. The working people realized that the state had broken the social contract, and dedicated themselves to passively sabotaging that state. Those who couldn't escape attempted to survive by working as little as possible. From the construction sector to the massive state bureaucracy, and even in agriculture, production fell alarmingly.

This was well known when the state-controlled labor union central, the Confederación de Trabajadores Cubanos Revolucionaria, met in its 39th conference in October 1979. The leaders of the Castroite workers' organization noted "a series of grave alterations in Cuban labor life." The hierarchs of the CTCR accused Cuba's workers of "lack of discipline, thefts, and negligence." They ended their analysis of the Cuban labor situation with some truly astonishing statistics. They stated that, "[Of] 1,600,000 persons in the active population (labor force), only half a million produce anything." That is to say, if we can trust these statistics, that less than a third of Cuba's labor force was participating usefully in the economy.

This data, obtained from a "Report of the Conference," couldn't be more revealing. It indicates that a majority of Cuba's workers, because of lack of motivation or some other reason, were refusing to work for "the construction of socialism"—a slogan that emanated constantly from the highest places in the dictatorship, and was repeated *ad nauseam* in every communications medium imaginable. The Cubans had lost faith in their government and would soon lose it in their country.

In 1982, the Cuban state put in place a law that permitted foreign companies, for the first time in over two decades, to invest in Cuba. This in large part corresponded to the Soviet New Economic Policy of the 1920s which, like the Cuban measure, was instituted for the purpose of avoiding "state decomposition." This policy of capitalist investment would, ironically, have a bright future in "socialist" Cuba.

The smaller scale agricultural reform of allowing "farmers' free markets" had a much darker future. Under this reform, the state allowed campesinos to sell some of their farm products directly to consumers outside of the state rationing system. It was motivated to permit this largely because of its own inability to reliably supply rationed products. This small-scale experiment was rapidly shut down by the government, which reasoned in the admirable style of scientific socialism—at the same time that it was encouraging investments by multinational corporations—that farmers' markets would create a dangerous petit bourgeoisie, in contradiction to the principles of revolutionary socialism.

The sociopolitical crisis of the USSR at the end of the 1980s, and the sad ending in 1991 of the system imposed on the Russian people by Lenin, had deplorable consequences for the Cuban economy. During the last five years of Soviet assistance, 1986–1990, economic aid averaged over $5 billion per year, a figure which was impossible to maintain by a disintegrating political system. The Castro regime decided to survive the socialist camp disaster by changing its political economy and entering into a "Special Period," which would lead to a social situation worse than anything that had gone before, and to a quality of life worse than that in Third World countries. (The "Special Period" is still in effect.)

To avoid anything similar to the "Bucharest Syndrome" (the shooting of the dictator by his own forces), the regime instituted even more repressive measures, increased the severity of the political laws, and targeted its own military. General Arnaldo Ochoa, a national hero of the African campaigns decorated as a "Hero of the Republic of Cuba," was, because of suspicion of disloyalty, condemned to death; he was shot by a firing squad on July 13, 1989. Colonel Antonio de la Guardia was shot on the same day, as were two other military officers, Amado Padrón and Jorge Martínez. Patricio de la Guardia, Antonio's brother, and a general with the elite Special Troops

(Tropas Especiales), was condemned to 30 years in prison. This purge of high-ranking military men ended in September 1989 with the arrest and sentencing of José Abrantes, a Ministry of the Interior (secret police) general. Abrantes died soon thereafter under mysterious circumstances while in prison.

At the same time that it was purging its military and secret police, the Castro regime initiated an opening in the direction of the so-called Cuban community in exile, particularly in the United States. This opening including permission for exiles to visit Cuba and to send money directly to their family members in Cuba. (Of course, money spent on travel and money sent to Cuban citizens would prop up the Cuban economy, and thus help prop up the Castro regime.) The Castro government also opened a strong diplomatic campaign to increase economic ties with all of the capitalist countries in Europe and Asia, as well as, surprisingly enough, the U.S., the Vatican, and Israel.

At the same time, and marking the definitive economic failure of Castro's "socialism," the farmers' markets were permitted to reopen; some establishment of privately owned small businesses was tolerated; and, most significantly, the "dollarization" of the Cuban economy took place. This last meant that the U.S. dollar could circulate just as freely in Cuba as it did in the U.S.—while up till this point trafficking in dollars meant going to jail in Cuba. The purpose of this measure was to expedite the sending of money by exiles to Cuba. This amount quickly reached $800 million per year, an amount higher than that produced by the most recent sugar crops (sugar being a badly decayed industry in Cuba).

Meanwhile the slogans about the "gains" realized in health and education were repeated, for external consumption, while class differences sharpened between those employed in Castro's apparatus, those receiving money from relatives abroad, and those relying on salaries paid in devalued pesos. Once again hopelessness spread like a cancer among the least favored and, as in not so remote times, the most daring Cubans decided to illegally abandon the island on flimsy rafts via the Straits of Florida—a very dangerous journey that has claimed thousands of victims over the years. In a very real sense this is a form of suicide induced by desperation, and a form in which Cuba leads the world. The Elian González affair is a good illustration of this tragedy.

Perhaps the worst incident in this ongoing sad situation was that involving the tugboat "13 de marzo" ("March 13th"). On July 13, 1994, more than 70 persons crowded this tug as it set sail from

Havana toward Florida. It was intercepted outside Havana Bay by the Cuban coast guard, which ordered it to return to Havana. The tug refused and continued heading toward Florida. At that point the Cuban coast guard vessel attacked the "13 de marzo" with high pressure water hoses, sinking it. Forty-one persons died when it went down, including many women and children. The survivors were taken prisoner. This sordid attack on unarmed civilians was supposedly ordered directly by Fidel Castro.

While all this has been going on, Castro has definitively ended his "socialist" experiment, with the sole purpose of maintaining his hold on power. He has instituted a form of state capitalism, similar to that of neo-fascist "Red" China, in which foreign investors in direct partnership with the Cuban state dominate the production of goods and services. As an example, the workers in the Cuban tourism industry, an industry entirely in the hands of the Cuban state and Spanish investors, receive their salaries in Cuban pesos (the exchange rate being about 20 pesos to one dollar), which effectively excludes them from the world of "dollarization." As well, the Cuban people in general are barred from entering the hotels and beaches reserved for foreign tourists, thus creating a type of apartheid—imposed by their "socialist" government.

This is a pathetic conclusion to a revolution that began amidst jubilation and great hopes. After 40 years the Cuban revolution has ended in economic deprivation, desperation, sharp class divisions, massive emigration, and a criminal tyranny that suppresses all dissent. How did this come to pass? How did this project that promised civil liberties, political and social reforms, just and honest government, and an equitable redistribution of the country's riches come to such a bad end? How did a revolution—and a "revolutionary" government —with great popular backing end up like this?

There are many reasons for this failure, but in our view there are two primary ones: the socioeconomic course and the speed with which it was adopted by Cuba's ruling elite; and the continual, massive repression of individual liberties.

In regard to the first of these, the transition from the capitalism that existed in Cuba prior to the revolution to the authoritarian pseudo-socialism substituted for it never yielded the expected results. This was largely due to the idiotic and ego-driven speed with which changes were implemented. The bearded ones were in too much of a hurry to impose their system, and never seriously planned the transition from one system to the other. But it was also due to the very nature of the "socialism" they attempted to impose. Instead of handing over the fields, factories, and workshops directly to the workers after expropriating them from their owners—a measure with which Cuba's anarchists would, of course, have been in accord—the Cuban government placed all of the great businesses, industries, banks, transportation networks, etc. under the control of the state. And they put elements loyal to the government, but without the foggiest idea of how to make these enterprises function, at the head of them all. It's not surprising that those without expertise in the fields they controlled made a hash of things, especially in that they were attempting to implement rapid structural change.

The second reason, perhaps more important than the first, was the creation of a military dictatorship worse than that which preceded it, a massive repressive system reaching into every neighborhood (via the CDRs), capable of violence and murder to maintain itself in power, and that mistreated, harried, and tortured political prisoners more savagely than its predecessors. Castro's and the PCC's destruction of individual liberties was a crime against the Cuban people, a people whose chronicle is that of love of liberty and fighting for freedom.

This destruction of personal freedom was the principal reason for the Communist disaster on the island. A shocked, enslaved people on their knees cannot effectively collaborate in social and political reconstruction. This is precisely why the many marxist attempts to create free, peaceful, egalitarian societies through the systematic use of coercion, violence, and terror by small elites have failed so abysmally the world over.

For their part, the Cuban anarchists have fought against tyranny throughout Cuban history, from the struggle against the repressive capitalism of the sugar barons to the pseudo-socialism of Castro. The anarchists were the first to understand and denounce the Castro regime. The anarchists' struggle for freedom and their understanding of what Castroism meant for Cuba can be seen as early as 1960 in Agustín Souchy's *Testimonios sobre la Revolución Cubana* and the public denunciation of Castro in the same year by the Asociación Libertaria de Cuba. The correctness of these early appraisals can be fully appreciated now that end of Castroism finally appears to be drawing near.

With Castro's death, there will be a new dawning of liberty in Cuba. That dawn will allow Cuba's anarchists to once again propagate anarchist ideas and to organize on the island. The solidarity of overseas anarchist groups will be an important help in those efforts, but it won't be indispensable. It will be Cuba's workers themselves who will organize to achieve freedom in its concrete sense of control over their own lives, control over the wealth they create, and control of the work that produces that wealth. As the old Asociación Internacional de los Trabajadores saying goes, "The emancipation of the workers must be the task of the workers themselves."

But Cuba's anarchists have pointed the way to that emancipation. Since the 19th century, they have fought a dual fight: against tyranny and for workers' control of the economy. In regard to Castro, Cuba's anarchists have consistently opposed his counter-revolution (suppression of individual freedom and the institution of state control rather than workers' control) since its early dark days. Remarkably early on Cuba's anarchists expressed their opposition to centralization, violence, coercion, and the remarkable militarization of Cuba (a matter on which many U.S. and European anti-militarists have been notably silent), and their support of worker-controlled unions, free municipalities, agricultural cooperatives, and collective workplaces.[1] To put this another way, Cuba's anarchists have consistently supported a real revolution rather than the phony one which has mesmerized so many leftists (including many anarchists).

Anarchism and its ideas are not dead in Cuba, as many who wish to erase these concepts of social redemption from the Cuban agenda wish us to believe. Marxism, as a utopia, as a vision of a better world, and as a practical means to get to that world, died when its ideas were put into practice by Lenin, Trotsky, Stalin, Mao, Kim Il Sung, Pol Pot, and Castro. The ideas of anarchism are, in contrast, quite alive—and they showed their vitality in the one major test to which they were ever put: the Spanish Revolution of 1936–1939. It is clearly premature to bury libertarian ideas.

Anselmo Lorenzo once said, "The first thing necessary to being an anarchist is a sense of justice."[2] We would add that it's also necessary

---

1. Incredibly, there still are a few examples of free cooperatives in Cuba, which the Castro dictatorship hasn't crushed. These are agricultural cooperatives located in remote, mountainous regions, which were organized around the beginning of the 20th century, and which the regime has largely ignored because of their relative inaccessibility. These cooperatives have continued to be productive—in contrast to the marked inefficiency of most of the rest of Cuban agriculture—and may well serve as useful models for a freer Cuba.

2. Anselmo Lorenzo was a Spanish anarchist and typesetter who wrote an influential-at-the-time book, *El Proletariado Militante* ("The Militant Proletariat"), and who founded several anarchist periodicals in Spain, including *El Productor* (not to be confused with the Cuban periodical of the same period), *Revista Blanca* ("White Review"), and *Tierra y Libertad*. He was active in the Spanish anarchist movement for over 40 years, and was a founder of the Confederación Nacional del Trabajo (CNT) in 1910.

to be an optimist. The new generation of Cubans, who have suffered the terrors of Castroism for decades, will find libertarian ideas to be the best, and probably the only, means of achieving a world free of intolerance, domination, hate, greed, and vengeance.

Optimism is a key factor in understanding the task of reconstructing anarchism in Cuba, in part because it's a key to Cuban psychology. But there are other psychological factors that must also be taken into account. One is the rampant ideological confusion and disillusionment on the island.

Marxists have always insisted that the correct path to socialism is the creation of an elite, a "revolutionary vanguard," that after taking power will lead the people to a socialist utopia by instituting "scientific" political and social principles. Of course, this approach has led to failure in virtually every land where the principles of Marx and Lenin have been put into practice. In Cuba, this attempt to produce a "new man" has led to disaster; the old revolutionaries were unable to force-produce a "revolutionary" youth.

The Cuban people have for nearly two centuries held in common a love of freedom. This first manifested itself in the struggle for independence from Spain, where some took the path of violent insurrection, others demanded reforms, and the majority simply wanted a better system of government that Spanish colonialism. Later, in the twentieth century, the failure of two republics semi-independent of the U.S., and the rise of two outright murderous regimes, those of Machado and Batista, didn't prevent the generation that came of age in mid-century from continuing the fight for Cuban freedom. But the defeat and humiliation of this idealistic, revolutionary generation by the at first authoritarian and later despotic figure of Fidel Castro placed a major roadblock in this centuries-old quest for liberty. If there's any positive aspect to the Castro dictatorship, it's that it has served as an object lesson to many Cubans to never support strongmen or "maximum leaders," no matter what "revolutionary" slogans they mouth.

But the Castro detour will be just that—a detour. There are many other social, moral, and psychological characteristics of the Cuban people that incline them instinctively, as it were, toward anarchism: their disrespect or indifference toward the state; their permanent rebellion against authority and its representatives, be they political or religious; and their systematic opposition to laws, rules, and regulations that attempt to restrict their freedom.

At the same time, it's necessary to point out that even though the Cuban character has an affinity for anarchism, being anarchic and being an anarchist are not the same thing. Still, Cubans are inclined to defy authority and to defy the laws of both church and state.

The Castro government was well aware of this Cuban tendency, and it took pains to suppress it from the start through the massive use of terror and coercion. The fear unleashed by Castro has temporarily dried up the love of liberty and the disdain for tyrants and their orders. The Cuba of today, with its multitude of prisons, secret police, and government informers on every block (the Committees for the Defense of the Revolution—more accurately, the Committees for the Defense of the Regime), is a society based on mere survival. Only through the use of near-infinite repression has Castro maintained his grip on power; and not only has he retained that, he's temporarily created a different Cuban attitude (at least as publicly expressed)— one that disdains "bourgeois civil liberties" and that respects repressive laws. In short, Castro's is a remarkable achievement: replacement of the traditional Cuban love of freedom by its opposite, cringing submission.

At the same time, while the present regime bears great responsibility for this "achievement," there were tendencies in this direction prior to the rise of Castro; and Cuba's anarchists, from the time of *El Productor*, have attacked these tendencies. First and foremost has been the matter of racism. Cuba (at the same time as Brazil) was the last country in the Western Hemisphere to abolish black slavery; and the racism and economic disparities left in slavery's wake were a severe hindrance to social emancipation in Cuba throughout the twentieth century.

The Castro regime has made much of its supposed elimination of racism in Cuban society, but in recent years racism has resurfaced, for economic reasons. Since the Castro regime reversed itself and allowed the free circulation of U.S. dollars on the island, and the sending of dollars from exiles (predominantly white Cubans) to those still in Cuba, a great many white Cuban families have been able to survive while doing very little or no work and, of course, while producing no useful goods or services. This has led to considerable resentment on the part of those not receiving money from abroad (primarily blacks), and it has also resulted in the introduction of a *de facto* class system with heavy racial overtones.

This class system has led to widespread indifference and indolence in agriculture and the sugar industry. Workers and campesinos refuse to work more than the absolute minimum necessary in a society where tourist dollars mean more than those produced by any type of production for export.

As for the means—other than coercion, violence, and surveillance —employed by the Castro government to keep itself in power, one must cite its propaganda apparatus. The Cuban government controls every radio station, TV station, and publication on the island. From these, the Cuban people receive a daily dose of marxist-leninist "scientific socialism," a doctrine with which they dare not publicly disagree. They also receive daily reports about how happy they are because of the revolutionary "gains" of the Castro regime, and because of their supposed "equality."[3] Hearing such claims repeated day after day, year after year, without public contradiction, some come to believe them. And others—primarily those in the government/Communist Party apparatus, the top tier in Cuba's class-based society—*want* to believe those claims, because they help justify their privileged positions.

Cuba's educational system also serves as an indoctrination factory. Students receive daily doses of marxism as revealed truth, and they are not free to criticize it, just as they are not free to criticize the educational system imposed on them by the state. They also are not free to choose their own paths in life. As in Plato's republic, if the state decides that they have, for example, an aptitude for veterinary medicine, they must serve the state as veterinarians. In education, as in virtually every other aspect of Cuban life, freedom is absent.

◆   ◆   ◆

Since remote times, human beings have evaluated, criticized, and altered the society that surrounds them. Anarchism is a recent development in this noble and humane undertaking, which has run as a thread through human history from the Athens of Socrates, to the Stoic philosophers, to the Renaissance, and to the philosophers and encyclopedists of the Enlightenment. William Godwin in England and P.J. Proudhon in France are but two early examples of those who took this tradition and built upon it to produce anarchism. If I read

---

3. The revolutionary "gains" trumpeted by the Castro regime become less impressive with each passing day. "Tropical socialism" is based on the U.S. dollar as the in-effect national currency, and the "socialist" Cuban regime has massive commercial traffic with almost every capitalist country except the U.S. It also engages in joint enterprises (especially in the area of tourism) with foreign corporations. In recent years, the "gains" it has produced include rapidly mounting unemployment and (for decades) mandatory "voluntary agricultural work." In regard to its primary piece of window dressing (for external consumption), its universal medical system is decades behind the developed world technologically, and the lack of necessary medicines has reached alarming proportions.

them correctly, their purpose, like that of later anarchists such as Errico Malatesta and Peter Kropotkin, was not only to eliminate the state, but to create a freer, more just human society. This intention—whether or not its bearers use the label "anarchist"—will, I am convinced, never die. It will continue to survive generation after generation, despite temporary setbacks, in Cuba as everywhere else.

As for Cuba, enchained and on its knees, I cannot help but think of the reference of Enrique Roig San Martín to the "tree of liberty." In Cuba, it put down roots and sprouted branches until, in the 1960s, it was burned and cut to the ground. But it didn't die. There will be those in the generations that succeed us who will take up the altruistic legacy of their forbears, so that the roots of anarchism, the roots of freedom, now buried in the fertile Cuban soil, will once again spring to life and will bear the fruits of liberty and social justice.

A Havana cigar factory around the turn of the 20th century.
El Productor and other anarchist periodicals reached
laborers in such factories through readers who
read aloud to the tobacco workers.

Enrique Roig San Martin

Enrique Creci

Enrique Messonier

Alfredo Lopez

Marcelo Salinas

Enrique Varona

Mastheads of four prominent Cuban anarchist periodicals

Casto Moscu

Manuel Gonzalez

Helio Nardo

Claudio Martinez

Juan R. Alvarez

Santiago Cobo

Bibliography

Agrupación Sindicalista Libertaria. *Declaración de Principios*. Editores Luz-Hilo: La Habana, 1960.

Aguirre, Sergio. "Algunas Luchas Sociales en Cuba Republicana." *Cuba Socialista*, 1965.

Asociación Libertaria de Cuba. *Memoria del II Congreso Nacional Libertario*. Editores Solidaridad: La Habana, 1948.

Avrich, Paul. *The Haymarket Tragedy*. Princeton University Press: Princeton, NJ, 1984.

Bakunin, Michael. *God and the State*. New York: Dover, 1970.

Bakunin, Michael. *Marxism, Freedom and the State*. London: Freedom Press, 1984.

Berkman, Alexander. *The Bolshevik Myth*. London: Pluto Press, 1984.

Berkman, Alexander. *The Russian Tragedy*. London: Phoenix Press, 1986.

Berkman, Alexander. *What Is Communist Anarchism?* New York: Dover, 1972.

Bookchin, Murray. *Post-Scarcity Anarchism*. San Francisco: Ramparts Press, 1971.

Bookchin, Murray. *Remaking Society*. Montreal: Black Rose, 1989.

Brinton, Maurice. *The Bolsheviks & Workers' Control*. London: Solidarity, 1970.

Buenacasa, Manuel. *El Movimiento Oberero Español*. Paris: 1966.

Bufe, Chaz. *¡Escucha Anarquista!* Mexico, DF: Ediciones Antorcha, 1987.

Bufe, Chaz. *A Future Worth Living*. Tucson, AZ: See Sharp Press, 1998.

Bufe, Chaz. *Listen Anarchist!* Tucson, AZ: See Sharp Press, 1998.

Bujarin, Nicolai y Fabbri, Luigi. *Anarquismo y Comunismo Científico*. Barcelona: Ediciones Sintesis, 1977.

Cabrera, Olga. *Alfredo López, Maestro del Proletariado Cubano*. La Habana: Editores Ciencias Sociales, 1985.

Cappelletti, Angel. *El Anarquismo en America Latina*. Caracas: Biblioteca Ayacucho, 1990.

Carrilo, Justo. Cuba 1933: *Estudiantes, Yanquis y Soldados*. Miami: Instituto de Estudios Interamericanos, University of Miami, 1985.

Casanovas Codina, Joan. *Bread or Bullets: Urban Labor and Spanish Colonialism in Cuba, 1850–1898*. Pittsburgh, PA: University of Pittsburgh Press, 1998.

Casanovas Codina, Joan. "El Movimiento Obrero y la Política Colonial Española en la Cuba de Finales del XIX." *La Nación Soñada:Cuba, Puerto Rico y Filipinas ante el 98*. Madrid: Ediciones Doce Calles, 1996.

Casanovas Codina, Joan. "El Movimiento Obrero Cubano, del Reformismo al Anarquismo." *Historia y Sociedad*. San Juan, PR: Departamento de Historia y Humanidades, Universidad del Puerto Rico, 1987.

Clark, Juan. *Cuba: Mito y Realidad*. Miami/Caracas: Saeta Ediciones, 1990.

Congreso Internacional de Federaciones Anarquistas. *Informe Carrara 1968*. Paris: Libraire Publico, 1968.

Dolgoff, Sam (ed.). *The Anarchist Collectives: Workers' Self-Management in the Spanish Revolution, 1936–1939*. New York: Free Life Editions, 1974.

Dolgoff, Sam (ed.). *Bakunin on Anarchy*. New York: Knopf, 1971.

Dolgoff, Sam. *The Cuban Revolution: A Critical Perspective*. Montreal: Black Rose, 1976.

Dolgoff, Sam. *Fragments: A Memoir*. London: Refract Publications, 1986.

Eichenbaum, V.M. ("Voline"). *The Unknown Revolution*. Detroit: Black & Red, 1974.

El Movimiento Obrero Cubano: Documentos y Artículos. Tomo I. La Habana, 1975.

El Movimiento Obrero Cubano: Documentos y Artículos. Tomo II. La Habana, 1977.

Esteve, Pedro. *Los Anarquistas de España y Cuba: Memorial de la Conferencia Anarquista de Chicago en 1893*. Paterson, NJ: El Despertar, 1900.

Fabbri, Luigi. *Bourgeois Influences on Anarchism*. San Francisco: See Sharp Press, 1987.

Fabbri, Luigi. *Influencias Burguesas sobre el Anarquismo*. Mexico, DF: Ediciones Antorcha, 1980.

Fernández, Frank. *Cuba, the Anarchists & Liberty*. Sydney: Monty Miller Press, 1987.

Fernández, Frank. *La Sangre de Santa Águeda: Angiolillo, Betances y Cánovas*. Miami: Ediciones Universal, 1994.

Ferrara, Orestes. *Una Mirada de Tres Siglos: Memorias*. Madrid: Playor, 1976.

Gambone, Larry. *Proudhon and Anarchism*. Montreal: Red Lion Press, 1996.

Goldman, Emma. *Anarchism and Other Essays*. New York: Dover, 1969.

Goldman, Emma. *Living My Life*. New York: Dover, 1970.

Goldman, Emma. *My Disillusionment in Russia*. New York: Apollo Editions, 1970.

Grobar, Fabio. "El Movimiento Obrero Cubano de 1925 a 1933." *Cuba Socialista*, 1966.

Guerra, Ramiro. *Manual de la Historia de Cuba*. Madrid: Ediciones R, 1975.

Guillame, James. *La Internacional de los Trabajadores*. La Habana: Ediciones de la Asociación Libertaria de Cuba, 1946.

Hidalgo, Ariel. "El Movimiento Obrero Cubano y el Primer Partido Anti-imperialista de la Historia." *El Caiman Barbudo*. La Habana: Segunda Etapa, 1974.

Iglesias, Abelardo. *Revolución y Dictadura en Cuba*. Buenos Aires: Editorial Reconstruir, 1963.

Kropotkin, Peter. *Anarchism and Anarchist Communism*. London: Freedom Press, 1987.

Kropotkin, Peter. *Fields, Factories and Workshops Tomorrow*. New York: Harper & Row, 1974.

Kropotkin, Peter. *Mutual Aid: A Factor of Evolution*. Boston: Porter Sargent, n.d.

Kropotkin, Peter. *The State: Its Historic Role*. London: Freedom Press, 1987.

La Enciclopedia de Cuba, Historia. Tomo IV. Madrid: Editorial Playor, 1974.

Launed, Carlos. *Definición del Sindicalismo: Sobre el Origen, la Conducta y la Misión del Militante Obrero*. Madrid: Fichas de Formación Libertaria, 1977.

Launed, Carlos. *El Anarcosindicalismo en el Siglo XX*. Madrid: Fichas de Formación Libertaria, 1978.

Le Riverend, Julio. "Raices del 24 de Febrero: La Economía y la Sociedad Cubana de 1878 a 1895." *Cuba Socialista*, 1965.

Leval, Gaston. *Collectives in the Spanish Revolution*. London: Freedom Press, 1975.

Leval, Gaston, Souchy, Agustín y Cano Ruiz, Benjamin. *La Obra Constructiva de la Revolución Española*. Mexico, DF: Editorial Ideas, 1982.

Litvak, Lily. *Musa Libertaria*. Barcelona: Antonio Bosch, 1981.

Malatesta, Errico. *Anarchy*. London: Freedom Press, 1984.

Martí, José. *Obras Completas*. La Habana: Editorial Nacional de Cuba, 1964.

Marrero, Leví. *Cuba: Economia y Sociedad*. Madrid: Editorial Playor, 1987.

Martinez Ortiz, Rafael. *Cuba: Los Primeros Años de Independencia*. Paris: Editores Le Livre Libre, 1964.

Maximoff, Gregory Petrovich. *The Guillotine at Work: The Leninist Counter-Revolution*. Sanday, Orkney: Cienfuegos Press, 1977.

Meltzer, Albert (ed.). *A New World in our Hearts: The Faces of Spanish Anarchism*. Sydney: Jura Press, 1977.

Miró, Fidel. *Anarquismo y Anarquistas.* Mexico, DF: Editores Mexicanos Unidos, 1979.

Molina, Juan M. *El Comunismo Totalitario.* Mexico, DF: Editores Mexicanos Unidos, 1982.

Moreno Fraginals, Manuel. *Cuba/España, España/Cuba.* Barcelona: Grijalbo-Mondadori, 1995.

Movimiento Libertario Cubano en Exilio. *Declaración de Principios.* Miami: 1965.

Olaya Morales, Francisco. *Historia del Movimiento Obrero Español.* Madrid: Madre Tierra, 1994

Ortiz, Fernando. *Contrapunteo Cubano del Tabaco y el Azucar.* Barcelona: Ediciones Ariel, 1973.

Peirats, José. *Anarchists in the Spanish Revolution.* London: Freedom Press, 1990.

Plasencia Moro, Aleida. "Historia del Movimiento Obrero en Cuba." *Historia del Movimiento Obrero en America Latina.* Mexico, DF: Siglo Veintiuno Editores, 1984.

Poyo, Gerald E. *José Martí: Architect of Social Unity. 1887–1895.* Gainesville, FL: University of Florida, Center for Latin American Studies, 1984.

Poyo, Gerald E. "The Impact of Cuban and Spanish Workers on Labor Organizing in Florida, 1870–1900." *Journal of American Ethnic History,* Vol. 5, No. 2, 1986.

Poyo, Gerald E. *The Anarchist Challenge to the Cuban Independence Movement, 1885–1890.* Pittsburgh, PA: University of Pittsburgh, 1985.

Rivero Muñiz, José. "La Lectura en las Tabaquerias." *Revista de la Biblioteca Nacional,* Oct.–Dic. 1951.

Rivero Muñiz, José. *El Movimiento Obrero durante la Primera Intervención.* Las Villas, Cuba: Universidad de Las Villas, 1961.

Rivero Muñiz, José. "Los Orígenes de la Prensa Obrera en Cuba." 1962.

Rivero Muñiz, José. *The Ibor City Story, 1885–1964.* Tampa, FL: 1976.

Rocker, Rudolf. *Anarchism and Anarcho-Syndicalism.* London: Freedom Press, 1988.

Rocker, Rudolf. *Anarcho-Syndicalism.* London: Phoenix Press, n.d.

Rocker, Rudolf. *Anarquismo y Organización.* Mexico, DF: Ediciones Antorcha, 1981.

Rocker, Rudolf. *En la Borrasca: Memorias.* Puebla, Mexico: Ediciones Cajica, 1962.

Rocker, Rudolf. *Nacionalismo y Cultura.* Puebla, Mexico: Ediciones Cajica, 1967.

Roig San Martín, Enrique. *El Productor.* La Habana: Consejo Nacional de la Cultura, 1967.

Serrano, Carlos. *Anarchisme et Independence á Cuba á la Fin du XIX Siecle*. Paris: Universite de Paris, 1986.

Shaffer, Kirwin R. Cuba para todos: Anarchist Internationalism and the Cultural Politics of Cuban Independence, 1898–1925. (forthcoming)

Souchy, Agustín. *Testimonios sobre la Revolución Cubana*. Buenos Aires: Editorial Reconstruir, 1960.

Thomas, Hugh. *Cuba or the Pursuit of Freedom*. London: Eyre & Spottiswoode, 1971.

Ward, Colin. *Anarchy in Action*. New York: Harper & Row, 1973.

Westfall, Glenn L. *Key West: Cigar City USA*. Key West, FL: Historical Key West Preservation Board, 1987.

Wexler, Alice. *Emma Goldman in Exile*. Boston: Beacon Press, 1989.

Zinn, Howard. *A People's History of the United States*. New York: Harper & Row, 1980.

Index